OPPOSING VIEWPOINTS® SERIES

Japan

D1300230

Other Books of Related Interest:

Opposing Viewpoints Series
America's Global Influence
Global Resources
World Religion

At Issue Series
Does the World Hate the U.S.?
United Nations

Current Controversies Series
Global Warming
Globalization

"Congress shall make no law . . . abridging the freedom of speech, or of the press."

First Amendment to the U.S. Constitution

The basic foundation of our democracy is the First Amendment guarantee of freedom of expression. The *Opposing Viewpoints* Series is dedicated to the concept of this basic freedom and the idea that it is more important to practice it than to enshrine it.

Japan

Karen Miller, Book Editor

GREENHAVEN PRESS
A part of Gale, Cengage Learning

GALE
CENGAGE Learning·

Detroit • New York • San Francisco • New Haven, Conn • Waterville, Maine • London

Christine Nasso, *Publisher*
Elizabeth Des Chenes, *Managing Editor*

For more information, contact:
Greenhaven Press
27500 Drake Rd.
Farmington Hills, MI 48331-3535
Or you can visit our Internet site at gale.cengage.com

For product information and technology assistance, contact us at

Gale Customer Support, 1-800-877-4253
For permission to use material from this text or product, submit all requests online at www.cengage.com/permissions

Further permissions questions can be emailed to permissionrequest@cengage.com

Articles in Greenhaven Press anthologies are often edited for length to meet page requirements. In addition, original titles of these works are changed to clearly present the main thesis and to explicitly indicate the author's opinion. Every effort is made to ensure that Greenhaven Press accurately reflects the original intent of the authors. Every effort has been made to trace the owners of copyrighted material.

Image copyright W.H. Chow, 2009. Used under license from Shutterstock.com.

LIBRARY OF CONGRESS CATALOGING-IN-PUBLICATION DATA

Japan / Karen Miller, book editor.
    p. cm. -- (Opposing viewpoints)
    Includes bibliographical references and index.
    ISBN-13: 978-0-7377-4372-2 (hardcover)
    ISBN-13: 978-0-7377-4371-5 (pbk.)
    1. Japan--Politics and government--1989- 2. Japan--Foreign relations--1989- 3. Japan--Social conditions--1989- I. Miller, Karen, 1973-
    DS891.J349 2009
    952.05--dc22
                                2009004705

Printed in the United States of America
1 2 3 4 5 6 7 13 12 11 10 09

Contents

Why Consider Opposing Viewpoints?   11

Introduction   14

Chapter 1: What Domestic Issues Face the People of Japan?

Chapter Preface   19

1. Japan Is Encouraging Population Growth   22
   Robert D. Retherford and Naohiro Ogawa

2. Japan Is Not Encouraging Population Growth   30
   Jane Ferretti

3. Women's Rights Are Respected in Japan   36
   Yoriko Meguro

4. Women's Rights Are Not Respected in Japan   42
   Satoko Kogure

5. Japan Is Becoming More Accepting   49
   of Immigrants
   Minoru Matsutani

6. Japan Does Not Accept Immigrants   55
   David McNeill

Periodical Bibliography   65

Chapter 2: What Global Role Does Japan Play?

Chapter Preface   67

1. Japanese Manufacturing Businesses   69
   Succeed Globally
   Jack Smith

2. Japanese Entertainment Businesses   77
   Suffer Globally
   Roland Kelts

3. Japan Has a Right to Preserve Its
   Whaling Heritage   88
   Colin Woodard

4. Japan Has No Whaling Heritage to Preserve   95
   Atsushi Ishii and Ayako Okubo

Periodical Bibliography   102

Chapter 3: How Does Modern Living Conflict with Tradition in Japan?

Chapter Preface   104

1. Entrepreneurs Are Succeeding in Japan   107
   Veronica Chambers

2. Business Traditions Cause Most Japanese   115
   Entrepreneurs to Fail
   The Economist

3. The Traditional Lifestyle Has Kept Obesity   125
   Low in Japan
   Benjamin Senauer and Masahiko Gemma

4. Modern Dietary Changes Have Created   131
   Obesity-Related Health Problems in Japan
   Rena Singer

5. Japanese Funerals Are a Standardized   136
   Social Ritual
   Andrew Bernstein

6. Pre-funerals in Contemporary Japan   144
   Satsuki Kawano

Periodical Bibliography   151

Chapter 4: How Does Japan Reconcile Its Past with Its Present?

Chapter Preface 153

1. Japan Has Not Fairly Compensated Its World War II Victims 155
   Eamonn Fingleton

2. Japan Has Officially Recognized the Rights of Its Indigenous People 164
   Mariko Sakai and Shozo Nakayama

3. Some Japanese Traditions Are on the Decline 171
   Anthony Faiola

4. Renewed Respect as Geisha Make a Comeback—and Take to Cyberspace 178
   Justin McCurry

Periodical Bibliography 183

For Further Discussion 184

Organizations to Contact 188

Bibliography of Books 196

Index 200

Why Consider Opposing Viewpoints?

> *"The only way in which a human being can make some approach to knowing the whole of a subject is by hearing what can be said about it by persons of every variety of opinion and studying all modes in which it can be looked at by every character of mind. No wise man ever acquired his wisdom in any mode but this."*
>
> John Stuart Mill

In our media-intensive culture it is not difficult to find differing opinions. Thousands of newspapers and magazines and dozens of radio and television talk shows resound with differing points of view. The difficulty lies in deciding which opinion to agree with and which "experts" seem the most credible. The more inundated we become with differing opinions and claims, the more essential it is to hone critical reading and thinking skills to evaluate these ideas. *Opposing Viewpoints* books address this problem directly by presenting stimulating debates that can be used to enhance and teach these skills. The varied opinions contained in each book examine many different aspects of a single issue. While examining these conveniently edited opposing views, readers can develop critical thinking skills such as the ability to compare and contrast authors' credibility, facts, argumentation styles, use of persuasive techniques, and other stylistic tools. In short, the *Opposing Viewpoints* Series is an ideal way to attain the higher-level thinking and reading skills so essential in a culture of diverse and contradictory opinions.

In addition to providing a tool for critical thinking, *Opposing Viewpoints* books challenge readers to question their own strongly held opinions and assumptions. Most people form their opinions on the basis of upbringing, peer pressure, and personal, cultural, or professional bias. By reading carefully balanced opposing views, readers must directly confront new ideas as well as the opinions of those with whom they disagree. This is not to simplistically argue that everyone who reads opposing views will—or should—change his or her opinion. Instead, the series enhances readers' understanding of their own views by encouraging confrontation with opposing ideas. Careful examination of others' views can lead to the readers' understanding of the logical inconsistencies in their own opinions, perspective on why they hold an opinion, and the consideration of the possibility that their opinion requires further evaluation.

Evaluating Other Opinions

To ensure that this type of examination occurs, *Opposing Viewpoints* books present all types of opinions. Prominent spokespeople on different sides of each issue as well as well-known professionals from many disciplines challenge the reader. An additional goal of the series is to provide a forum for other, less known, or even unpopular viewpoints. The opinion of an ordinary person who has had to make the decision to cut off life support from a terminally ill relative, for example, may be just as valuable and provide just as much insight as a medical ethicist's professional opinion. The editors have two additional purposes in including these less known views. One, the editors encourage readers to respect others' opinions—even when not enhanced by professional credibility. It is only by reading or listening to and objectively evaluating others' ideas that one can determine whether they are worthy of consideration. Two, the inclusion of such viewpoints encourages the important critical thinking skill of objectively evaluating an author's credentials and bias. This evaluation will illuminate an author's reasons for taking a particular stance on an issue and will aid in readers' evaluation of the author's ideas.

It is our hope that these books will give readers a deeper understanding of the issues debated and an appreciation of the complexity of even seemingly simple issues when good and honest people disagree. This awareness is particularly important in a democratic society such as ours in which people enter into public debate to determine the common good. Those with whom one disagrees should not be regarded as enemies but rather as people whose views deserve careful examination and may shed light on one's own.

Thomas Jefferson once said that "difference of opinion leads to inquiry, and inquiry to truth." Jefferson, a broadly educated man, argued that "if a nation expects to be ignorant and free . . . it expects what never was and never will be." As individuals and as a nation, it is imperative that we consider the opinions of others and examine them with skill and discernment. The *Opposing Viewpoints* Series is intended to help readers achieve this goal.

David L. Bender and Bruno Leone,
Founders

Introduction

> "While . . . it is not quite correct to say that the civilized world knows nothing of Japan, it may truly be asserted that what is known is very much less than what is unknown."
>
> —Francis L. Hawks,
> Narrative of an American Squadron
> to the China Seas and Japan, 1856

It is said—by Westerners—that Japan is the only "Western-ized" nation of the East. The people of what used to be called the Orient have long been objects of fascination to Europeans and North Americans and have been portrayed as magical and sage and inscrutable ever since Marco Polo published his travelogues in the 1200s. Since then, the stories about the mysteries of the East have permeated history, literature, and film. Despite the fact that Japan has adopted the political, social, and economic structures of the Occidental (Western) world, it still attracts attention from the West. For example, a few years ago a string of horror movies in the Japanese style (J-Horror) thrilled audiences. Translations of Haruki Murakami's novels have appeared on best-seller lists in the United States. Business publishers release books promising corporate success by following Japanese business principles (especially Toyota's). Educators turn their eyes to the Japanese school system to learn how to raise the test scores of American students. When the Japanese economy entered a recession, markets worldwide heeded it like prophecy and sought in it solutions to their own problems. Even the traditional Japanese diet purportedly guarantees longevity.

Of course, while many cultural ideas are shared, Japan and its people are still thought of by many as incomprehensible or as subjects to be mocked. The 2003 Sofia Coppola film, *Lost in Translation*, presented Tokyo as exhilarating, but impenetrable and ultimately isolating. The cable network Spike TV airs a show called *MXC*, which takes footage from the Japanese game show *Takeshi's Castle* and dubs it into English with no regard for what the Japanese hosts or participants are really saying. It is funny, but it is fantasy. The Japanese people on the show are obviously enjoying themselves as much as the American narrators and audience seem to be, but they are laughing at different jokes.

One hundred and fifty years ago, it was understandable that the people of Japan and the people of the Western Hemisphere would not understand each other. Japan had a long history of political and social isolation from other countries, and most of the nation was officially closed to trade and correspondence with citizens of other countries. The arrival of American naval officer Commodore Matthew Perry in 1854 put an abrupt (and not universally welcome) end to Japan's isolationist practice. By 1858, Japan and the United States had signed a treaty that allowed for the exchange of diplomats, trade, and the limited residence of Americans in Japan. But ensuing events hindered relations between Japan and the West. The rapid modernization of the country triggered internal conflicts and social upheaval and even brought new deadly diseases to the island, such as cholera. War with Britain broke out during the 1860s, and in 1868 the foundation for what became the Empire of Japan—the great Axis force in the Pacific during the Second World War—was laid. Only since the 1950s, when the United States compelled the defeated Japanese government to change by pushing them through the process of writing a parliamentary Constitution that undercut the monarchy, have the Western industrialized nations and Japan been communicating with any degree of mutual understanding.

So is it still reasonable to say that what is known about Japan is much less than what is unknown? Probably not. Hundreds of thousands of people from Japan and the rest of the world have participated in cultural, social, and business exchanges, and a network of beneficial relationships crosses the globe. Many of Japan's newspapers have regularly published English-language editions, and even its government Web sites have English-language pages. Information flows in and out of Japan by the minute. There are few secrets left. So why the continued scrutiny? Why does the idea of Japan still resonate as exotic and unknowable? The Japanese people have fashion, arts, food, and technology in common with the rest of the world. Baseball is practically the national sport. Then why is Japan swathed in a such a mystique? Why is it such a source of fascination?

At the heart of the matter is the question of whether the nation of Japan is more similar than dissimilar to the nations of the Western world. On the surface, Japanese people struggle with the same local and personal issues that every person struggles with in the industrialized world, from dealing with crabby coworkers, to protecting the environment, to finding self-fulfillment and true love. Beneath the surface is a history that does not stem from the shared Judeo-Christian values of European culture and the Greco-Roman philosophies of the ancient world. But there appear to be universal truths about the nature of human existence; it may not matter very much whose ancestor practiced Buddhism and whose ancestor practiced Christianity. After all, the Wii Fit console game sold out immediately in stores in Japan and in the United States. How different could the people of these two nations be?

Despite its sometimes contradictory reputation as a proud, technologically savvy, imperturbable, peaceful, warlike, traditional, and/or quirky nation, Japan faces the same conflicts and struggles with the same dilemmas that beset other industrialized societies. *Opposing Viewpoints: Japan* explores some of the supposed contradictions of this Westernized Eastern nation and describes in four chapters some of the strategies and approaches the Japanese people and government have devised to address their communal problems: What Domestic Issues Face the People of Japan? What Global Role Does Japan Play? How Does Modern Living Conflict with Tradition in Japan? and How Does Japan Reconcile Its Past with Its Present? Even though Japan may face some issues specific to that nation, its people also experience troubles and happiness in ways familiar to those in many other parts of the world.

CHAPTER 1

What Domestic Issues Face the People of Japan?

Chapter Preface

There is a relatively new ailment in Japan called "Retired Husband Syndrome." First described in 1991 by physician Dr. Nabuo Kurokawa, the syndrome strikes not husbands but the wives of Japanese men who are on the verge of retirement. Symptoms can include rashes and ulcers, as well as overt signs of depression. After a lifetime spent running a home in their husbands' absence (because work and career expectations kept the man away from the family), wives dread the round-the-clock presence of a man used to dictating from afar the rules of the household and demanding attention from the women in it. Compounding the problem is the fact that so few Japanese adults now are marrying and having children, so the multigenerational support group for catering to the retired husbands is missing from the wives' lives, as well as the fact that Japanese people have the longest life expectancy in the world. A man who retires at age 65 could live another thirty years. Middle-aged women ponder what it will be like to spend the last three decades of life under heavy domestic obligation—and they get sick.

Hardly surprising is the fact that divorce rates have skyrocketed for couples who have been married twenty years or more—these rates have as much as quadrupled in the past ten years. Divorce laws changed in 2007 to allow a divorced wife to collect up to 50 percent of her husband's pension. Despite the appearance of many support groups and "household training" classes for men who want to learn to help their wives, many women have had enough and leave the marriage.

In another country a rising divorce rate among retirees might be a socially lamentable but economically irrelevant matter, but it is fast becoming a financial crisis in Japan. The steep decline in birth rates and the increasing life expectancy for the elderly means that very soon there will not be enough young people to support the elderly, either with taxes, with family ties, or even with paid assistants. Strict immigration policies discourage young workers from settling permanently and starting families (which would supply workers and raise the nation's fertility rates), and social government programs that support the older generations, like health insurance, could run out of money. Several generations of older people will need assistance of some kind or another, and population projections suggest that assistance will be scarce.

In part, marriage means that two people can share household expenses. It also means that one nurse or one light housework helper can help two people with one visit. If the money available—privately and publicly—for services has been split between two households and if support workers are in short supply, the rising divorce rate may have serious social ramifications beyond the mental health of divorcees and the social impact of split families. Not only will the cost of medical and daily assistance increase for people who have, as a group, less individual income, but there also will be far fewer people getting even basic help. Often the difference between independent living and paying for long-term residential care is hiring someone with strong arms and a good back to help with the grocery shopping or cleaning the house every few weeks. Within the next few decades, unless population demographics change drastically, there may not be enough young people to hire for this work.

Marriage, of course, is not the only domestic arrangement that enables people to share living expenses. Some people will be able to live in their children's homes; others will find roommates. And of course not every retirement-age married couple will divorce, especially not among the younger generations who were raised on principles of gender equality. The changing corporate culture and the growing number of entrepreneurs means that fewer spouses will be completely estranged from each other at retirement age. Still, the divorce rate among retirees could cause serious problems that need to be addressed immediately.

The following chapter identifies other social crises and conflicts that face the nation of Japan, as well as the policies that have been enacted in an effort to defuse them.

> *"We are being strongly called upon to halt the decrease in children by creating an environment where parents can feel secure in giving birth and raising children."*

Japan Is Encouraging Population Growth

Robert D. Retherford and Naohiro Ogawa

Robert D. Retherford is the coordinator of Population and Health Studies at the East-West Center and an affiliate graduate faculty in sociology at the University of Hawaii. Naohiro Ogawa is a research adviser at the Advanced Research Institute for the Sciences and Humanities at Nihon University in Japan. The following viewpoint discusses various "pronatalist" policies enacted in Japan, which include the programs and incentives designed and implemented to encourage Japanese women and men to have more children.

As you read, consider the following questions:

1. What percentages of men and women does the Japanese government hope will start taking advantage of their entitled childcare leave, according to the authors?

Robert D. Retherford and Naohiro Ogawa, "Japan's Baby Bust: Causes, Implication, and Policy Responses," *The Baby Bust: Who Will Do the Work? Who Will Pay the Taxes?* Edited by Fred Harris, Rowman and Littlefield, Copyright 2006. Reprinted by permission.

2. According to Retherford and Ogawa, how are marriage statistics related to a decline in fertility in Japan?

3. What is the reasoning behind the proposal for six years of childcare leave for women in the Japanese workforce, as reported by the authors?

In 2002 the government announced a plan on "Measures to Cope with a Fewer Number of Children Plus One." The "plus one" plan argued that an important reason why fertility has continued to decline, despite the government's efforts to raise it, is that husbands are not doing enough to help with childrearing. The phrase "plus one" means that the effort to raise marital fertility should be strengthened, and that a greater role for husbands in childrearing should be a major component of this increased effort. The plan said that fathers should take at least a five-day leave when a child is born. It also said that, among regular full-time workers eligible for childcare leave, at least 10 percent of men and 80 percent of women should take childcare leave. The targets of 10 and 80 percent were based on a survey in which, among persons with young children, 7 percent of men and 76 percent of women said that they would take childcare leave if there were less social disapproval of childcare leave by employers and co-workers. The plan also said that there should be provisions for flex-time and shorter hours for couples with pre-school children, and it called for a target of 25 percent of eligible couples (husband or wife) working shorter hours. . . .

Legislation Is in Place

Following the issuance of the "plus one" plan, two laws were enacted in July 2003 in order to implement the goals set forth in the plan: (1) the Law for Measures to Support the Development of the Next Generation and (2) the Law for Basic Measures to Cope with a Declining Fertility Society.

The Law for Measures to Support the Development of the Next Generation (the "next generation" law) became effective on 1 April 2005, and will remain in effect for ten years. The law pertains only to firms with more than 300 workers on the payroll (including part-time workers and full-time contract workers). Within these firms, the law covers not only regular full-time employees but also all other employees who have been working continuously for more than a year, regardless of whether they are full-time or part-time and regardless of the length of their contracts. Each employer falling under the law is asked to prepare a plan to raise fertility among its employees. The plan must include targets, and it had to be submitted to the prefectural government by the time the law went into effect on 1 April 2005. There are no penalties for not coming up with a plan, but if the employer does not do so, the government can send the employer a notice urging the employer to take action. (In Japan such urging by the government is usually quite effective, although less so than previously because of less government leverage over business as a consequence of reductions in government regulation as part of the on-going restructuring of the economy.) The submitted plan must span at least two years but no more than five years. If the plan is approved, the employer receives permission to use a special logo that the employer can display on products, advertisements, and other promotional literature. At the end of the plan, the employer has to report progress under the plan to the prefectural government. The Labor Bureau of the prefectural government evaluates the plan with guidance from the national government's Ministry of Health, Labour, and Welfare. If progress is evaluated as unsatisfactory, the firm can no longer use the logo.

Goals for the Next Generation

The goals of the "next generation" law are mostly the same as those laid out in the "plus one" report a year earlier. The main targets are that, among eligible workers in eligible firms and organizations, 10 percent of men and 80 percent of women should take the childcare leave to which they are entitled. The main intent of these targets, and of the plans that had to be submitted by 1 April 2005, is to change the workplace atmosphere so that parents, and especially women, feel more comfortable about taking the childcare leave to which they are entitled. According to the 2002 round of the government's Basic Survey of Female Employment Management (firm-level reporting), among eligible workers in eligible firms, only 0.3 percent of men (compared with the target of 10 percent) and 64 percent of women (compared with the target of 80 percent) had taken childcare leave. The "next generation" law also sets a target that 25 percent of firms with more than 300 employees should have policies that allow women with pre-school children to work shorter hours.

In December 2004, the Childcare and Family Care Leave Act was revised to bring it into line with the "next generation" law, which specifies that all part-time workers and full-time contract employees who have worked continuously at a firm for more than a year are to be included in a firm's plan to raise fertility. The revised Childcare and Family Leave Act went into effect on 1 April 2005. Before this revision, temporary workers (including part-time workers and full-time contract workers) were not entitled to childcare leave.

The Law for Basic Measures to Cope with a Declining Fertility Society (the "basic measures" law), also enacted in 2003, states, "We are being strongly called upon to halt the decrease in children by creating an environment where parents can feel secure in giving birth and raising children who will be the next generation of society, and to realize a society in which children grow up equal and healthy in mind and body, and parents truly feel pride and joy." This law contains general language that appears to be intended to set the stage for future government action, but the law does not indicate specific actions to be taken. The specific actions are contained in the "next generation" law that was passed at the same time in July 2003.

Cash for Babies in Yamatsuri, Japan

After Hiroko Honda gives birth to her third child . . . she'll get a gift from the local government. . . .

Desperate to reverse a falling birth rate and a declining population, this town of 7,000 [in 2005] began offering rewards to persuade local women who have at least two children to have more: Yamatsuri pays them $9,200 per birth—half three months after the baby's arrival, the rest over the next 10 years.

Paul Wiseman,
USA Today, *July 28, 2005.*

The government [implemented a] New Angel Plan for 2005–2009. The general goals are the same as those in the "next generation" and "basic measures" laws of 2003. A major objective is to increase husbands' involvement in childcare and household chores. . . . According to background information included in the plan, men in their 30s with a child less than 5 years old spend an average of 48 minutes a day on childrearing and household chores. The plan sets a goal of raising that to two hours a day (two hours being about average for other economically advanced countries). Additional background information contained in the plan is that 23 percent of husbands in their 30s work more than four hours of overtime per day, resulting a total workweek of more than 60 hours. The plan sets a target of reducing this percentage by half by the end of 2009. The plan also calls for a further increase in the number of family support centers from 368 in 2005 to 710 by 2010 (at that time covering almost a quarter of the more than 3,000 administrative districts in the country). . . .

Encouraging Marriage Earlier and More Often

Increases in the mean age at marriage and the proportion never marrying account for about half of Japan's fertility decline since 1973. This suggests the need for policy initiatives aimed at improving the functioning of the marriage market.

One way that has been tried is dating services, which were pioneered in Japan, but so far only in the private sector. At the present time there are about 3,100 dating services firms in the country. As a service to their employees, some large firms contract with dating services firms, and these large firms sometimes cooperate with each other in providing these services. For example, the Mizuho Financial Group (formerly the Fuyou Family) contracts collectively with a dating services firm for their employees. The Mizuho Financial Group is a large industry group, or *keiretsu*, that includes Mizuho Bank, Hitachi, Canon, Sapporo Beer, Marubeni, NKK Steel, and a number of other major corporations. For an employee in one of the group's companies to get the services, he or she must join the Fuyou Family Club and pay an annual membership fee of 50,000 yen ($500), plus another 70,000 yen ($700) if a marriage results. These rates are subsidized by the companies and are low compared with the fees that individuals must pay if they deal directly with a dating services firm. The Fuyou Family Club claims 7,000 members and a 10 percent success rate in terms of matches that result in marriages. Most other large industry groups have similar out-sourcing arrangements with dating services firms.

The Japanese government may soon get involved in matchmaking by providing government support for dating and related services. On 24 January 2005, the Ministry of Economy, Trade and Industry held its first expert group meeting to investigate the possibility of government support of "marriage information services," including not only dating services but also "life support" services such as training to improve interpersonal communication skills. . . .

Who Should Carry the Burden?

Japan's Childcare and Family Care Leave Act allows up to one year of childcare leave to care for an infant under one year of age, but most women would probably consider that one year of childcare leave is not enough. Although data are not available on this point, it seems likely that most Japanese women would prefer to have two children in fairly quick succession, with about a three-year interval between them, and then return to work when the youngest child is about three years old, when the mother would feel more comfortable about putting the child in a day-care facility. In other words, most women would probably prefer a six-year leave. This is probably why [an earlier analysis] that simulated the opportunity cost of children under different scenarios specified a six-year period for temporarily dropping out of the labor force to have children.

Requiring employers to grant six years of childcare leave with return rights and other benefits would, however, place a very heavy burden on employers. (The government is currently considering extension of the leave to three years.) The problem of the length of the leave highlights the dilemma facing policymakers, which is how to implement two major imperatives:

- Restructuring the Japanese economy to be more efficient and competitive in the global economy

- Restructuring Japanese society to be more marriage-friendly and mother-and-child-friendly in order to raise fertility

The trick is how to do this so that the second imperative does not undermine the first, and without jeopardizing women's hard-won gains in education and employment. Experience to date suggests that this will not be easy, and that it will be very costly to both the government and firms to raise fertility back up to the replacement level.

| *"Many people do not think [Japanese] birth rates will increase unless there are also social and cultural changes."*

Japan Is Not Encouraging Population Growth

Jane Ferretti

Jane Ferretti is an instructor at the School of Education at the University of Sheffield in the United Kingdom. She teaches geography, supervises student teachers, and provides professional development to established teachers. She also is an editor of the magazine Wideworld, *which targets geography students in graduate study programs. The following viewpoint discusses some of the reasons that fertility rates are declining in Japan and speculates on the possible negative social and economic outcomes that could result if the government and people of Japan do not act quickly to change the situation.*

As you read, consider the following questions:

1. Why are Japanese women having so few children, according to Ferretti?

Jane Ferretti, "Japan's Ageing Population: Population Studies Are an Important Part of Many GCSE Courses. This Case Study Looks at a Country with a Declining and Ageing Population," *Wideworld*, Vol. 18, No. 4, April 2007, pp. 8–10. Copyright © 2007 Philip Allan Updates. Reproduced by permission.

2. What are some economic reasons that Japanese people have so few children, as reported by the author?

3. What is one immediate solution to the impending labor shortage in Japan, according to Ferretti?

Japan has a population of about 127 million, the tenth largest in the world, but it is unusual because its population is declining. Only a few other countries (such as Italy, Germany and Russia) have declining populations, but none is predicted to fall as rapidly as the population of Japan.

Japan has approximately 27 million elderly people and the largest proportion of over-65s of any country (21%). It also has the smallest proportion of people under the age of 15 (13.6%), which will result in huge difficulties for Japan in the future, as the number of working people will be unable to support the population. These changes are happening more quickly in Japan than in Europe or the USA and could seriously affect the economy of one of the world's wealthiest countries.

Why Is the Population Declining?

Japan's population grew rapidly as it industrialised in the early twentieth century, increasing from 60 million in 1926 to 100 million in 1967. Since the 1980s, however, population growth has slowed and, having peaked in 2005, it is now in decline. Estimates suggest that the population will fall to 121 million by 2025 and 100 million by 2050. What is more worrying is that the proportion of old people will increase, and by 2030 it is estimated that one person in three will be over 65. This will put great strain on the country. . . .

The main reason for the decline in numbers is that Japanese women are not having enough children. Many Japanese are choosing to marry at a later age, on average between 28 and 30 years old, and this means that they have children later, or not at all. Many women also decide not to get married, choosing to study or pursue a career instead of having children.

In Japanese culture bringing up children is usually left to the mothers. Very few men take any childcare leave (although they are entitled to do so), and surveys reveal that over 40% of fathers have never changed a nappy [diaper] or put the children to bed. This fact, and the lack of childcare facilities, means that few women return to work after having their children, and many other women feel they would have to give up too much in order to have a family.

There are also strong economic reasons why people choose not to have children or to have only one or two. Being pregnant in Japan is expensive, as pregnancy is not covered by health insurance. This means that women must pay for their own medical care during pregnancy, including hospital checkups. After the birth, healthcare is only provided free for infants up to the age of three (or five in some areas). Added to this are the huge costs of schooling and university education, and many families decide they can only afford to have one or two children at the most. Child benefit paid by the government to families is low and hardly enough to pay for nappies, let alone all the other costs associated with having a family.

Does a Decline Matter?

There are two particular problems that will result from the declining population. The first is the cost of looking after people as they get older and the second is the lack of younger workers to fill jobs.

As more and more people reach retirement age, the country will have to find more money for their pensions. This has already meant raising the retirement age and obtaining higher contributions from both employers and employees, and it will have to be reviewed again in the future. Already there is evidence of older people working in shops, at the main airports,

A Baby Bust

In the aftermath of World War II, the rush to build a modern economy sparked migration from rural towns such as Nishiki to Japan's urban centers. But officials say the lure of the big city is no longer the key factor driving depopulation. For at least the past decade, the leading cause of the town's shrinking population base has been a disturbingly low birthrate.

Last year [2004], 42 babies were born in Nishiki, the lowest number since the town was incorporated in the 1950s, while 75 villagers died, according to local statistics. Nishiki's plight, analysts said, could be an omen of Japan's future. . . .

Japan's disappearing schools are emblematic of the problem. More than 2,000 elementary, junior high and high schools nationwide have been forced to close over the past decade. The number of elementary and junior high students fell from 13.42 million in 1994 to 10.86 million [in 2004]. An estimated 63,000 teachers have lost their jobs.

Anthony Faiola,
Washington Post, *March 3, 2005.*

on the Tokyo subway or driving taxis. In the future there will be a great strain on the country as it tries to provide adequate healthcare to support the elderly. This will inevitably mean larger tax bills for people who are working.

The second and more immediate problem is that businesses are finding it difficult to recruit new staff, and this will become even harder in the future. If the jobs cannot be filled, then the productivity of the country will fall and so will its prosperity.

What Is Being Done?

In the long term, it is hoped that Japanese women can be persuaded to have more children, but social attitudes and trends are difficult for the government to tackle. Reforms such as increasing the amount of child benefit, providing tax allowances for families and making childcare more accessible are being considered, in the hope that this will increase birth rates. However, many people do not think birth rates will increase unless there are also social and cultural changes.

In the short term, Japan must solve its labour shortage. One obvious way is to encourage more immigration. At the moment there are only about 2 million foreigners living in Japan, and this is nowhere near enough. Workers are needed in a whole range of jobs, including dirty or dangerous jobs that Japanese people do not want to do (such as cleaning or working in residential homes) and jobs for which people need to be highly skilled and trained.

Shortages in Japan's computer engineering and programming sector are well known. Some estimates say that Japan will need as many as 500,000 migrants each year for the next 40 years in order to keep pace.

The difficulty with this, however, is that the Japanese as a nation are opposed to immigration. Japanese-born people make up 98.5% of the population, and it is difficult for foreigners to be accepted or to become Japanese citizens. In comparison, in Switzerland 18% of the workforce is foreign.

Although the Japanese government is considering how to encourage more migrant workers it also wants to impose controls on immigration. It will be difficult to change the views of most Japanese people, who fear that migration threatens what they consider to be the purity of the Japanese culture.

There is no doubt that Japan's population is in decline and, although the government is aware of this problem, many feel it has been slow to react. It is unlikely that the smaller and increasingly elderly population will be able to maintain the country's productivity and prosperity, unless steps are taken to address the issues of population decline.

"Japan will promote and implement policies enhancing both the status of women and gender equality within and outside our nation."

Women's Rights Are Respected in Japan

Yoriko Meguro

Yoriko Meguro is a professor of sociology at Sophia University in Tokyo, Japan, and the Japanese representative to the United Nations Commission on the Status of Women (CSW). The following viewpoint is the transcription of the speech she delivered at the fiftieth session of the CSW. In it she enumerates Japan's achievements and its ongoing challenges in the arena of women's rights and equality. Though it still has room for improvement, she notes, Japan has come a long way in respecting the rights of women.

As you read, consider the following questions:

1. What general goals does Meguro say are set by the Second Plan for Gender Equality to be achieved by 2010?

Yoriko Meguro, "Statement by Dr. Yoriko Meguro, Representative of Japan, at the Fiftieth Session on the Commission of the Status of Women" (New York), *The Ministry of Foreign Affairs of Japan*, March 1, 2006, p. 1–4. Copyright © 2006 The Ministry of Foreign Affairs of Japan. Reproduced by permission.

2. What percentage of researchers in the natural sciences would the Japanese government like to be women, according to the author?

3. According to Meguro, how did the percentage of women participating in Japanese government councils and committees change from 1975 to 2005?

Encouraging gender equality is an integral part of the structural reform being carried out by Prime Minister Junichiro Koizumi. In this connection, in October of [2005] Prime Minister Koizumi appointed [Professor] Kuniko Inoguchi as Minister of State for Gender Equality and Social Affairs, the first ministerial post to deal exclusively with these issues.

As a result of the general election that took place in September 2005, there are now an unprecedented number of female members of the House of Representatives—forty-three, an increase by twenty-six percent. While women's participation in society is growing and more women are involved in decision-making processes, the proportion of the whole they represent remains unsatisfactory. Japan therefore will continue to vigorously promote gender equality and undertake, reforms to create a fair-society in which both men and women can fully exercise their capacity to achieve self-fulfillment.

One of the specific measures Japan has taken was its revision of the Basic Plan for Gender Equality at the end of [2005].... The new Second Plan covers comprehensive measures to be implemented before the end of fiscal year 2010, such as setting a numerical target for the percentage of women in managerial positions in every field and applying temporary special measures for attaining those goals, as well as setting an additional numerical target for female scientists, and enhancing measures to support them in their research activities.

In this statement, I would like to outline what Japan has achieved and the challenges it faces in the area of gender equality especially with regards to the two themes of the current session of the Commission [on the Status of Women (CSW)]. Let me turn to the first theme: "Enhanced participation of women in development." . . .

Expanding Women's Roles

In the field of education, Japan has taken measures to enhance opportunities for women to engage in life-long learning and career training, including providing support for women who, having retired from the workforce once to have a family, wish to undertake a second career, and for those trying to balance their career and the responsibility of raising a family. A particular target has been the enhancement of women's participation in the fields of science and technology. Furthermore, considering the remarkably low proportion of women engaged in research in Japan compared to other countries—only 11.9 percent—the government has, for the first time, under the initiative of the Minister of State for Gender Equality to work in close cooperation with the Council for Science and Technology Policy, set in the Second Plan and elsewhere, a numerical target of achieving 25 percent of women in the field of natural sciences.

In the field of health, Japan is taking measures to provide maternal and child health care services that continue through all periods from pregnancy to delivery, and also health education and counseling, in order to ensure that women remain healthy throughout their lives. Comprehensive measures to address HIV/AIDS have also been taken, including assurance of medical care, testing and consulting services as well as dissemination of information on how to deal with the virus.

In the area of work, Japan has developed administrative guidance and methods of providing assistance to settle disputes and helping private companies to take positive action for equal employment opportunities. In addition, the government has promoted plans to support those balancing work and family responsibilities and provided information services and training programs to help rural women engaged in agriculture improve their technical and management skills so that they can enhance their economic status.

Japan has implemented international and domestic measures to increase women's participation in development. To this end, Japan announced the "Initiative on Gender and Development" at the last session of the CSW, through which it is attempting to integrate gender perspective into every phase of Japan's ODA [Official Development Assistance] implementation and strengthen ODA assistance to developing countries making efforts to achieve gender equality and empower women. In the policy formulation process, Japan takes into consideration women's need to have access to basic social services in the areas of education and health and also to have access to equal employment opportunities.

Although there continue to be numerous challenges to efforts to ensure a positive environment in the fields of education, health and work, Japan renews its commitment to further implement its current policies.

A Call for More Women Leaders

I would now like to turn to the second theme: "Equal Participation of women and men in decision-making processes at all levels." For the realization of a gender-equal society, it is essential to ensure equal participation and to maintain a democratic system in which everyone's views are given proper opportunities to be reflected.

In Japan at the time of the First World Conference on Women in 1975, the proportion of females in the national advisory councils and committees stood at only 2.4 percent. As a result of promoting measures to achieve the "30 percent target as soon as possible but no later than the end of fiscal year 2005," this figure has risen to 30.9 percent, a success that was achieved half a year ahead of schedule.

A Powerful Japanese Woman

Since becoming chief of Japan's largest grocery store chain, Daiei, [in 2005,] Fumiko Hayashi hasn't had an easy ride. Daiei struggled under the weight of billions of dollars in debt, as well as challenges from other home-grown retailers. Hayashi enacted a plan to shutter money-losing stores and pare down debt. But the chain still has a long way to go: Though the company turned a profit after posting losses [in 2005], sales as of February [2006] were down 9% from the previous year. The daughter of a vegetable broker, Hayashi got a job after high school as a secretary. Then she began working at a Honda car dealership in the late 1970s, where it is said that she broke the dealership's one-month sales record. She later became head of sales at BMW Japan. After taking the top job at Daiei, whose president is male, Hayashi told Japanese newspaper *Nikkei Weekly*: "I thought I would be able to create an example of a success in male-female collaboration . . . that would be a good model for Japanese women to follow. That sense of a mission was the biggest factor prompting me to take up the position."

Susan Kitchens, "The 100 Most Powerful Women: #39 Fumiko Hayashi," Forbes, August 31, 2006. Copyright © 2006 Forbes, Inc. Reproduced by permission.

The level of women's participation in decision-making processes in Japan, however, is still very low. There has been, in general, little improvement at any level, national or local, public or private. It is essential to enhance women's participation in all the areas that touch on daily life, in response to changes that have taken place in socio-economic conditions.

Recognizing these obstacles, the revised Basic Plan for Gender Equality clearly stipulates that greater participation by women is necessary in the fields of environment and disaster prevention and recovery. Moreover, the Plan clarifies the 30 percent target that was set for the proportion of leadership positions women should occupy in all fields of society by 2020. Japan will undertake an initiative to promote the "temporary special measures" defined in its Basic Law for a Gender-Equal Society, and will support local governments and Private enterprises as they take appropriate measures to encourage further participation by women in decision-making.

Equality at Home and Abroad

To conclude, Japan will promote and implement policies enhancing both the status of women and gender equality within and outside our nation, and it will do so in close partnership with international organizations and civil society, including NGOs [nongovernmental organizations]. Japan also deems it important to establish partnerships that extend beyond borders. In this connection, we would like to propose to hold a meeting . . . in Tokyo at the ministerial level, hosted by Prof. Kuniko Inoguchi, the Minister of State for Gender Equality, in cooperation with the national machineries of our Asian neighbors in particular, in order for us to exchange our views on policies on gender equality.

| *"Gender stereotypes that pose difficulties for women who aspire to achieve equal rights and opportunities remain widely accepted in Japan."*

Women's Rights Are Not Respected in Japan

Satoko Kogure

Satoko Kogure is a writer on Japanese political affairs and military history and a columnist with The Japan Times. *The following viewpoint urges the people of Japan not to revise Article 24 of the Japanese constitution, which was written and ratified under the direction of the United States at the end of World War II and which provides for equal rights for women. Article 24 was not, in the end, revised (though other articles were), but the controversy that grew out of the proposed revision highlights the conflicts regarding women's place in Japanese society and the reasons why women's rights, especially, need to be legally protected.*

As you read, consider the following questions:

1. What does Article 24 of the Japanese constitution say, as cited by the author?

Satoko Kogure, "Turning Back the Clock on Gender Equality: Proposed Constitutional Revision Jeopardizes Japanese Women's Rights," *The Asia-Pacific Journal: Japan Focus*, May 22, 2005, p. 1–4. Copyright © 2002–2008 JapanFocus.org. Reproduced by permission.

2. How do the proposed changes to Articles 9 and 24 reinforce traditional gender stereotypes, in Kogure's opinion?

3. On average, how do women's salaries in Japan compare with men's salaries, according to the author?

As the government emphasizes patriotism as part of the national school curriculum and discussion continues apace over revising Article 9 [of the Constitution], some Liberal Democratic Party (LDP) lawmakers are calling for changes to the Constitution that may put equal rights and individual freedom at risk.

The ongoing discussion on revising the Constitution has grown to include calls for amendments to Article 24—the clause protecting gender equality in postwar Japan—in a bid to lock conservative family values into the legal and social framework at the expense of individual freedom.

[In] June [2004], an LDP Constitution revision panel introduced a plan to revise Article 24, which took effect in May 1947, "from the viewpoint of stressing the value of family and community."

However, this has sparked a storm of protest, mainly among women and defenders of human rights, who argue that the panel's suggestions are aimed at assigning fixed gender roles in society so as to return to a pre-war social model and force women to stay in the home.

Values vs. Freedoms

Article 24 states that "laws shall be enacted from the standpoint of individual dignity and the essential equality of the sexes."

But the LDP panel held that "'individualism' has come to mean 'egoism' in postwar Japan, leading to the collapse of family and community."

Arguing that the Constitution should maintain traditional values and morals that they believe were neglected when the

Constitution was drafted by occupation forces after the war, the panel implicitly laid the blame for postwar 'egoism' at the feet of Japanese women who have chosen careers and independence over early family life and child-rearing.

The panel's appreciation for traditional values is itself rooted in an admiration for the Japanese self-sacrificing attitude.

"It's a matter of course that the mother had a primal responsibility for her child," says LDP panel member Nishikawa Kyoko who herself raised two children as a full-time housewife.

"Complaining about fixed gender roles is so nonsensical," she says. "It's a simple fact that men and women have essential roles based on their sex. Only women can bear a child. Criticizing sex roles is weakening women's minds. Mothers should naturally appreciate their responsibilities toward their own children."

She believes that this feeling has been lost by some Japanese mothers. "But this responsibility is not shared by all of today's mothers. It's very irresponsible that today's mothers just have a child and don't fully take care of it. Expressing the value of family in the Constitution is my message for those mothers."

Codifying Traditional Roles

However, the concept of "essential gender roles" was long the basis for justifying gender inequality, confining women to the home and denying them public roles. By the same token, when individuals are defined primarily as one member of a family, women's rights and freedoms will always be at risk under the pretext that women have roles that only women can play.

University of Tokyo Professor Takahashi Tetsuya believes that recent ruling party moves to alter the Constitution are troubling. "While women are expected to maintain the family and take care of children and the elderly, men are expected to support the country," he says. "Today's discussion on Article 24 is closely connected to the discussion on Article 9, the war-renouncing provision. As the LDP panel suggested in its report, since the constitutional provisions under discussion now specify people's responsibility to defend the country, they need people for the front. This is viewed as the man's role."

The panel's efforts are not simply designed to undermine equal rights. Rather they seek to produce individuals suited to the government's needs, he believes. "In this sense," he says, "individual dignity, which is stipulated in Article 24, would be undermined by assigning fixed sex-roles. The government is trying to change the national character by sacrificing the individual's rights for the family and, by extension, the family for the country."

It was precisely this form of pre-war social model, that is, the devoted mother serving her husband, who in turn unquestioningly served the emperor on behalf of empire and war—that prompted the inclusion of Article 24 in the postwar Constitution in the first place.

Beate Sirota Gordon, who drew up Article 24 as a civilian member of the General Headquarters [GHQ] of the Allied Forces in 1946, says that the clause was essential to progress in postwar Japan. "I saw that Japanese women—my friends and acquaintances—had no rights, so I tried to include as many women's rights as possible in the Constitution," she said during a visit to Tokyo.

Controversial from the Start

Gordon remembers that the Japanese government was fiercely opposed to Article 24 in discussions with GHQ. "There was a harsh objection to the gender-equality provision from the Japanese side, just as they were opposed to the emperor's status change," she says.

The United Nations Global Gender Empowerment Measure (GEM)

Country	GEM Ranking
Norway	1
Sweden	2
Finland	3
Denmark	4
Iceland	5
Netherlands	6
Belgium	7
Australia	8
Germany	9
Canada	10
Japan	**54**

TAKEN FROM: The United Nations Development Program, "Human Development Report 2007/2008." www.undp.org.

Interestingly, Gordon's original draft of Article 24 did include a reference to family values—"The family is the basis of human society and its traditions for good or evil permeate the nation"—which was removed from the final version. In fact, however, Gordon's view of family and individual differs sharply from that of the LDP panel. While Gordon viewed the family as based on "individual dignity and the essential equality of the sexes," the panel's aim to prescribe individual responsibility to sustain the family poses a direct threat to individual rights, notably those of women.

Dismayed at efforts to alter articles 24 and 9, Gordon says: "Both Article 9 and 24 are needed for world peace. There are many oppressed women in the world. Japan should be proud of its Constitution, and other countries should follow the Japanese model."

Indeed, Article 24 of today's Constitution has helped post-war Japanese women gradually achieve important status and social protections in several areas.

A Constant Struggle

The legislative by-products of the provision include the Equal Employment Opportunity Law (1986), the Basic Law for a Gender-Equal Society (1999) and a Law for the Prevention of Spousal Violence and the Protection of Victims (2001). The Equal Employment Opportunity Law was revised in 1997 to prohibit discrimination against women at all stages of employment.

Nevertheless, the impact of these legal developments has been relatively limited. While women accounted for 41.1% of the country's total employment in 2004, 39.9% of these employed women worked part-time, accounting for 69.3% of all part-time workers. Part-time workers are paid only 65.7% of full-time workers, and receive limited rewards. This is among the important causes of the high wage gap between sexes in Japan; the average female earned 67.6% of the pay of the average male in 2004.

In the United States, female share of the total employment in 2004 was 46.5%, and approximately 26% of these women worked part-time. With more participation in full-time work, the median wage of women in the United States was 80% of the wages of men. Likewise, the participation of part-time workers among working women in most European countries was far lower than that in Japan and the wage gap between sexes was smaller with women earning 81.8% of men's wages in the United Kingdom (2004), 85.8% in France (2004) and 74.0% in Germany (2003). In these countries, the wage gap between female full-time workers and part-time workers was also smaller: female part-time workers earned 74.5%, 81.7%, 87.5% of the wages of full-time female workers in the United Kingdom (2000), France (1994), and Germany (1995) [respectively].

Article 24 Is Important

However, despite the gaps in legislation and the persistence of differences in work and income patterns between men and women, the progress in Japan's legal framework in the last decades still deserves attention. The above-mentioned legislation was based on the constitutional guarantee of gender equality.

That provision itself was an achievement rooted in modern history. As Gordon observes, "Japanese women, who had been struggling for their rights in pre-war time, deserved and realized Article 24." The pioneers of the Japanese feminist movement include Kishida Toshiko and Kageyama Hideko of the Meiji era (1868–1912), and Hiratsuka Raicho and Ichikawa Fusae, who fought for women's suffrage, equal opportunity in education, and protection of motherhood in the democratic movement of the Taisho era (1912–1926). Although Gordon consulted European models such as the Constitution of the Weimar Republic and those of the Scandinavian countries when drafting the provision, her proposal included women's rights and protections that earlier Japanese feminists had been calling for.

Despite these developments over a century, however, Japanese lawmakers have recently come under attack for failing to adequately promote awareness of equal rights. For example, a report issued by the Committee on Elimination of Discrimination against Women of the United Nations [in 2003] "stressed the importance of sensitizing and training public officials and members of the judiciary to eliminate gender-biased stereotypes."

In spite of the constitutional provision and subsequent laws and social movements, gender stereotypes that pose difficulties for women who aspire to achieve equal rights and opportunities remain widely accepted in Japan. Revising Article 24 of the Constitution will provide a setback for those aspiring to gender equality.

> "We will accept immigrants, not foreign workers, and let them live in Japan permanently."

Japan Is Becoming More Accepting of Immigrants

Minoru Matsutani

Minoru Matsutani is a resident of Japan who was educated in the United States. He has written for a variety of publications, including the Chicago Sun-Times *and* Bloomberg News, *and is a staff writer for* The Japan Times, *a daily English-language newspaper. The following viewpoint, taken from an article that appeared in the latter publication, discusses a plan that aims to bring ten million immigrants into Japan during the next fifty years, as well as to increase the number of foreign exchange students and refugees. The proposed plan attempts to address an anticipated labor shortage as Japan's population ages and birth rates decline.*

As you read, consider the following questions:

1. According to Matsutani, how would the proposed plan change the way immigrants to Japan are treated?

Minoru Matsutani, "Radical Immigration Plan under Discussion," *The Japan Times*, June 19, 2008, p. 1–3. Copyright © The Japan Times. All rights reserved. Reproduced by permission.

2. How would the proposed immigration plan change citizenship laws, in the author's opinion?

3. What are some fears about increasing the number of immigrants in Japan, noted by Matsutani?

Foreigners will have a much better opportunity to move to, or continue to live in, Japan under a new immigration plan drafted by Liberal Democratic Party [LDP] lawmakers to accept 10 million immigrants in the next 50 years.

"The plan means [that some politicians] are seriously thinking about Japan's future," said Debito Arudou, who is originally from the United States but has lived in Japan for 20 years and became a naturalized citizen in 2000. "While it is no surprise by global standards, it is a surprisingly big step forward for Japan."

The group of some 80 lawmakers, led by former LDP Secretary General Hidenao Nakagawa, finalized the plan on June 12 [2008] and aims to submit it to Prime Minister Yasuo Fukuda. . . .

The plan is "the most effective way to counter the labor shortage Japan is doomed to face amid a decreasing number of children," Nakagawa said.

Helping Immigrants Settle In

While establishing an environment to encourage women to continue to work while rearing children is important to counter the expected labor shortage, bringing in foreign workers is the best solution for immediate effect, said the plan's mastermind, Hidenori Sakanaka, director general of the private think tank Japan Immigration Policy Institute.

"We will train immigrants and make sure they get jobs and their families have decent lives," Sakanaka said in explaining the major difference between the new plan and current immigration policy. "We will take care of their lives, as op-

Expanded Citizenship Rights

In a ruling sure to affect thousands of others born out of wedlock to non-Japanese mothers, the Supreme Court [in June 2008] granted 10 children of Filipino women the right to Japanese nationality....

In overturning the high court decision, Supreme Court Chief Justice Niro Shimada ruled that the provision in the law resulted in "discrimination without any rational reason" and thus violated Article 14 of the Constitution, which stipulates equality under the law.

Jun Hongo,
Japan Times, *June 5, 2008.*

posed to the current policy, in which we demand only highly skilled foreigners or accept foreigners only for a few years to engage in simple labor."

Japan had 2.08 million foreign residents in 2006, accounting for 1.6 percent of the population of 128 million. Raising the total to 10 million, or close to 10 percent of the population, may sound bold but is actually modest considering that most European countries, not to mention the U.S., have already exceeded this proportion, Sakanaka said.

Fukuda outlined in a policy speech in January [2008] his aim to raise the number of foreign students to 300,000 from the current 130,000, but without specifying a timetable.

However, the immigration plan calls for the goal to be achieved soon and for the government to aim for 1 million foreign students by 2025. It also proposes accepting an annual 1,000 asylum seekers and other people who need protection for humanitarian reasons.

Advancing Human Rights

Akio Nakayama, manager of the Tokyo office of the Geneva-based International Organization for Migration, said the important thing about the new plan pitched by the LDP members is that it would guarantee better human rights for immigrants.

"The plan emphasizes that we will accept immigrants, not foreign workers, and let them live in Japan permanently," Nakayama said.

"The most remarkable point is that immigrants' family members are included," he said. "I have never seen this in similar proposals."

Also, he praised the plan for proposing changes to the resident registration law to allow children born in Japan to foreign parents to have Japanese citizenship. Under the current Nationality Law, one of the parents must be Japanese and the parents must be legally married for their children to have Japanese citizenship.

This provision, however, was recently ruled unconstitutional by the Supreme Court, allowing 10 children born to Filipino mothers and Japanese fathers out of wedlock to gain the right to Japanese nationality.

The plan also includes establishing an entity to be called the Immigration Agency to integrate related duties that are now shared by multiple government bodies.

Among other proposals, the plan calls for extending the maximum duration of student and working visas to five years from the current three, easing the conditions for granting permanent resident status, setting up more Japanese-language and culture centers overseas and outlawing racism.

Establishing Legal Protections

Arudou, a foreigners' rights activist, noted the importance of establishing a legal basis for specifically banning discrimination against non-Japanese.

"Founding a legal basis is important because people do not become open just because the government opens the door," he said.

Also under the plan, the foreign trainee program, which supports Japanese companies and organizations that hire foreigners to work up to three years in Japan, would be abolished. Some trainees who have come to Japan under the program have sued their employers, claiming they have been abused with minimal pay and harsh working conditions.

This set of bold proposals appears positive, but Minoru Morita, a political critic at Morita Research Institute Co., doubts Nakagawa's plan will be formally adopted by the LDP anytime soon.

"Expanding immigrants to this large of a scale may cause social instability," he said. "Nakagawa will face difficulty gaining support from LDP colleagues and ministry officials."

He added that Nakagawa may have come up with the plan because he could be angling to become the next prime minister and would therefore want to stand out with a bold policy proposal. "Nakagawa may have to water down the proposals," Morita said.

Anticipating Opposition

Fears over the consequences of bringing in more foreigners are probably shared by many in a country where people consider themselves highly homogeneous.

"Immigrants surely bring dynamism to the Japanese economy, as well as crime," said a researcher at a public entity studying crimes committed by foreigners. The researcher asked not to be named.

While the researcher admitted immigrants would be better treated if the new plan were adopted and thus their motivation for committing crimes would decrease, he added: "But what if they lose their jobs? What if the economy worsens? We cannot take better care of unemployed immigrants than Japanese because we should treat them equally."

Goro Ono, author of *Bringing Foreign Workers Ruins Japan*, does not think bringing in immigrants is necessary.

Ono, an honorary professor at Saitama University, said he does not believe Japan is facing a labor shortage now or in the future.

"If industries where labor is in high demand pay adequate salaries, people will work there," he said.

Ono said nursing is a good example. Japan is actively bringing in Indonesians and other foreigners to cover a dire shortage because nurses here are woefully underpaid, he said, while on the other hand public entities never have trouble finding garbage collectors because they get decent salaries.

Ono also brought up the lack of discussion about the cost of preparing the infrastructure to accept more immigrants.

Sakanaka is ready to face such criticism just as all revolutionaries have in the past. His proposals would shake up Japan from the inside and it would be a historical moment if they all became law, he said.

"The Meiji Restoration was the first stage in opening up the country to foreigners," he said. "Now we are entering the second stage."

> *"The vast majority of universities in [Japan] will not hire or even consider foreigners for tenured positions, regardless of language level, publication record, and teaching ability."*

Japan Does Not Accept Immigrants

David McNeill

David McNeill earned his doctorate studying the Japanese information society. He taught at universities in Ireland and England before taking a position at Sophia University in Tokyo. He is currently a coordinator for the peer-reviewed online journal Japan Focus as well as a journalist for a variety of publications around the globe. In the following viewpoint, McNeill describes the experiences of many foreign instructors at Japanese universities who are long-term residents of that nation but who are treated as temporary guests at best and unwanted interlopers at worst. He argues that Japan's homogeneous approach to education limits its success and cooperation in the world community.

David McNeill, "Still Foreign after All These Years," *The Chronicle of Higher Education*, Vol. 53, No. 24, February 16, 2007, p. A47. Copyright © 2007 The Chronicle of Higher Education. This article may not be published, reposted, or redistributed without express permission from The Chronicle.

As you read, consider the following questions:

1. What is one explanation for why Japanese universities are not considered prestigious worldwide, in McNeill's opinion?

2. According to the author, why were Japanese universities not hiring full-time foreign professors before the 1990s?

3. What is one significant obstacle to implementing an "internationalized" university in Japan, according to Mc-Neill?

One way of taking the educational pulse of Japan is to visit the School of International Liberal Studies here at Waseda University. Higher education seems cosmopolitan and vibrant at the school, with a faculty that is 30 percent foreign—drawn from a dozen nationalities—offering a diverse curriculum taught in English to students who must spend a year abroad to graduate. And the dean is British.

As a fluent speaker of Japanese who was the most senior academic on the staff, Paul Snowden was the natural choice for the job. But his appointment as dean [in 2006], the highest position reached by a non-Japanese at Waseda, the country's top private university, was considered so unusual that he compared it to the first moonwalk.

"For Waseda the smashing of this glass ceiling might be seen as a pretty huge step," he told the *Asahi Shimbun* newspaper.

Indeed, Waseda's embrace of foreigners is still much more the exception than the rule in Japan. Few Japanese universities have been as ready to take the hammer to tradition. While some parts of society are slowly opening up—the number of permanent foreign residents recently passed two million, or 1.57 percent of the total population—universities in this Asian superpower remain strikingly homogenous and isolated from the globalizing trend in higher education.

A Closed Community

According to the Ministry of Education, just 5,652 of the 158,770 professors employed in Japanese higher education are foreigners on full-time contracts, mostly at private universities. Most of those foreigners work as low-level English-language teachers on short-term contracts.

And although Japan has finally reached its target, set in 1984, of enrolling 100,000 foreign students every year, the bulk of them are from China and South Korea. That means the rest of the world sends fewer than 20,000 students to Japanese campuses each year. In contrast, Japan sends nearly 40,000 students a year to the United States alone.

Many Academics and administrators here agree that Japan's insular higher-education system would benefit enormously by opening up to the rest of the world. They cite such problems as the sluggish adoption of new course-management technologies like Blackboard's, the lack of creative thinking in departments and classrooms, and a shortage of programs for older students. Critics add that most Japanese universities are not competitive internationally: Just three Japanese institutions made the top-100 list in the 2006 rankings of the *Times Higher Education Supplement*, in London.

"Japanese universities are not doing well, and one reason is because the education students are getting is homogenous," says Bruce Stronach, an American who, as president of Yokohama City University, is probably the highest-placed foreigner in Japanese academe. "They're not getting a diversity of view's—the ability to argue and discuss and that sort of Socratic give-and-take with their colleagues."

Bern Mulvey, an American who is dean of Miyazaki International College, which runs one of the handful of continuing-education programs on the large southern island of Kyushu, says that when he raised the idea of starting such programs among his colleagues, he was greeted with astonishment.

"They'd never heard of it until I explained it to them," he says. "Finding solutions in universities often involves listening to the faculty members from Romania or Nicaragua or other places who have new ideas. In Japan those voices would not be heard."

Time to Diversify

The education ministry appears to agree with such criticism, increasingly sprinkling the buzzword "internationalization" in documents on university reform, and proclaiming, at least officially, that more foreign academic talent is welcome here.

Japan's top campus administrators are reading from the same page.

"Universities have to internationalize for the sake of diversity," says Hiroshi Komiyama, president of the elite University of Tokyo—which employs just 250 foreign nationals among its 5,000 faculty members. "People who are part of the same culture and language can no longer really develop intellectually."

His own university's poor record of hiring foreigners is largely the result of external forces, he explains. "A lot of this is not our fault," he says. "National public universities were banned from employing foreigners full time until the 1990s because employees were classed as civil servants." Those rules were only recently relaxed.

Underlying Tensions

Pull back the curtain, however, and major obstacles to reform emerge. Except at a handful of prestigious academic citadels, say professors, university administrators keep foreigners on a very short leash, hiring them only on contracts lasting three years or less, and dictating what they can teach. Faculty positions in Japan are still rarely advertised outside the country, unless universities are looking for foreign-language instructors. And the few job advertisements that are posted internationally often demand that highly qualified applicants agree to spend much of their time correcting the English-language papers of Japanese colleagues, say foreign professors.

Many foreign academics here say they have been discriminated against: snubbed in corridors, passed over for promotion in favor of Japanese colleagues, and worse.

"I was at a university where female faculty members would get off the elevator and take the stairs," says Mr. Mulvey, of Miyazaki. "They said they didn't want to be alone with a foreigner because you didn't know what was going to happen."

Negative feelings among foreigners can run deep. At a recent conference on education issues here, foreign professors compared themselves to lab animals. "When they have been sufficiently abused or have mastered the maze, it is time to bring in a 'fresh specimen,'" one said. Some have sued their employers for discrimination. Several institutions, including the prestigious private Ritsumeikan University, are dealing with disputes involving foreign instructors.

Limited Progress

Nonetheless, a growing number of foreign professors are climbing the slippery academic pole in Japan. Foreigners now run research projects, departments, and even universities, evidence for Mr. Snowden, of Waseda, that the system is changing.

Still, he says, his own promotion to dean has put him under special scrutiny. "I've really got to perform well," he says. "Otherwise there will be this excessive interpretation of a foreigner having done badly, and never electing another one."

Mr. Snowden, who is knowledgeable about teaching English as a second language and has written about comparative linguistics and culture, joined Waseda as a part-time instructor in 1980. Like many successful foreign academics in Japan, he questions whether non-Japanese have always made the commitment needed to build university careers here.

Discrimination Against Foreign Renters

Im [Yeong Eun], 25, together with two South Korean friends who also came to Japan ... visited three real estate agencies to rent an apartment in Shinjuku Ward. But the agencies turned them away because they were foreigners. . . .

According to a 2006 survey conducted by Tokyo-based nonprofit organization Information Center for Foreigners in Japan, 94 percent, or 220 respondents, out of 234 foreigners in Tokyo who visited real estate agents said they were refused by at least one agent.

Akemi Nakamura, Japan Times, *November 10, 2007.*

Linda Grove, a former dean of liberal arts at Tokyo's Jesuit-run Sophia University, which has the highest percentage of non-Japanese staff of any university in the country—over 50 percent—argues that language has been a huge problem.

"It was very difficult for Japanese universities to take on people who couldn't attend meetings or read documents," she says. "I don't think it was because they didn't want foreigners. It was worrying that they could cope."

Sophia's school of liberal arts is one of the few in Japan that offer an entire curriculum in English and have a campus that boasts a fair number of non-Asian faces. In the corridors here, English is heard as commonly as Japanese, and doors have nameplates for professors from all over the world.

Internationalized Universities

In contrast, most university campuses in Japan are still strikingly monocultural. The faculty at the University of Tokyo for example, looks much as it did two decades ago.

"Many Japanese students have never even talked to somebody from outside the country," says Igo Takahiro, a first-year student. "It would obviously be better for our education if we had more opportunities to learn what foreigners think and exchange ideas with them. I think most of my friends would agree."

Some academics believe that Sophia could serve as a model of the "internationalized" university, with its mix of teaching styles and polyglot community of Chinese, Koreans, Americans, and Europeans. Few Japanese students, however, speak and read English well enough to be able to function in such an environment. Tom Gill, an associate professor in the department of international studies at Meiji Gakuin University, says his department would like to hire more foreign academics but cannot: "Finding a guy who has a specialty other than Japanese is not easy." Many universities argue that hiring more non-Japanese simply increases the workload for current staff members.

Such claims infuriate equality campaigners. "Yes, poor Japanese-language skills are an issue," says Mr. Mulvey, who is a fluent Japanese speaker and reader. "However, this really is beside the point. The real problem is that Sophia University and the few places like it are exceptions. The vast majority of universities in this country will not hire or even consider foreigners for tenured positions, regardless of language level, publication record, and teaching ability."

The "embarrassingly" low number of tenured foreign professors in Japan bears that out, says Mr. Mulvey. The education ministry cannot even say how many foreigners are tenured, arguing that tenure is a matter for each institution to take up. "We don't know how many Japanese are tenured, either," says a ministry spokesman.

While the government does run a few programs intended to recruit foreign academics, the spokesman notes that "we cannot order universities to hire more foreigners."

For some, this response proves that the government is not serious about internationalizing higher education or discouraging discrimination. "This is an intensely political issue," says Debito Arudou, a naturalized Japanese citizen and lecturer who says universities are "systemically denying" tenure to non-Japanese academics through the use of employment term limits.

Discrimination Is Apparent

Ivan P. Hall, one of Japanese academe's fiercest critics and author of *Cartels of the Mind: Japan's Intellectual Closed Shop*, a 1997 book that argues that Japan has put up institutional barriers to outsiders in the media, academic, and legal sectors, says the lowly position of most foreign academics in Japan is by design. "The ministry knows universities discriminate against foreigners and so it lies about these statistics," he says. "Every time you try to nail this thing down it is like jelly."

Japanese universities, he says, have a long record of banishing *gaijin*, foreigners, to the academic sidelines. The record, he says, can be read only as a determination—conscious and politically motivated—not to open up to foreign scholars. It is a system of apartheid that keeps most gaijin "disenfranchised and disposable."

University administrators say it is difficult to find qualified foreigners, but that they are trying. "If they can work the same as a Japanese person, and if they are comfortable with the language, we hire the foreigner," says Takuya Honda, a professor in the School of Knowledge Science at the Japan Advanced Institute of Science and Technology.

Administrators also reject the idea that the government forces them away from such hires, and that there are any systematic efforts to keep out foreign academics. "I have no idea what the Ministry of Education thinks," says Mr. Komiyama, president of the University of Tokyo. "We don't consult with them when we want to hire more people from abroad."

Mr. Snowden, dean of international studies at Waseda, acknowledges that some of the hiring criteria can be tough to meet. "Japanese universities are wary of committing themselves to people who claim they might stay but who take off after a few years," he says. "I was told when I became full-time that I must stay 10 years or 'we're not interested.' Foreigners sometimes don't stay around for very long."

Rhetoric vs. Reality

Government rhetoric often seems least convincing in universities outside the big cities, where a multicultural dawn looks far off indeed. The school of humanities at Hokkai Gakuen University, in Sapporo, for example, employs just one tenured professor among its 36 foreign academics despite its efforts to build a Sophia-style humanities program. Now the university is in a dispute with a foreign instructor who says he was passed over in favor of a Japanese colleague.

"It's a bit uncomfortable, but management said all foreign teachers should be on one-year contracts," says Toshikazu Kuwabara, dean of the school. The university introduced the measure, he says, because it has had "problems" with foreigners, including sexual harassment of students and difficulty in getting along with one another in campus housing.

"We've had to put them into separate apartments, and that kind of thing is difficult to arrange," the dean says. Four of the instructors speak very little Japanese, he adds, "even after 10 years."

The issue of the treatment of foreign faculty members recently became quite public, and acrimonious, at Akita International University, in northern Japan. Promoted as one of the new "internationalized" campuses, the university had agreed to retain about a dozen foreign lecturers after the local prefecture took over the campus from the Minnesota State Colleges and Universities system in 2003.

The instructors, some of whom have been living in the area for a decade and a half, say they were led to believe that their contracts would be extended, but were stunned when told at a meeting [in] July [2006] that they would not have jobs as of March [2007].

Instead, the university told them, their positions would be advertised internationally, in an attempt to recruit the strongest candidates. Some of the instructors were replaced by other foreign academics, but those who were let go find it ironic that, after years of hearing complaints that foreign instructors don't understand Japan and are too transient, a university would dismiss academics with deep roots in the community. They also note that the new president of the university, Mineo Nakajima, is on the prime minister's education-reform council.

"The idea universities are internationalizing is ridiculous," says one of the instructors, Mark Cunningham, who taught English. "They want the distinguished-visitor model rather than someone who disrupts the status quo. It is not a two-way exchange."

Periodical Bibliography

Hannah Beech
"The Wasted Asset: Japanese Women Are Smart and Entrepreneurial, So Why Is So Little Effort Made to Harness Their Talents?" *Time International*, August 29, 2005.

Dennis Behreandt
"The Japanese Robot Revolution," *New American*, November 13, 2006.

Christopher Bjork and Ryoko Tsuneyoshi
"Education in Japan: Competing Visions for the Future," *Phi Delta Kappan*, April 2005.

Christian Caryl and Akiko Kashiwagi
"The Gap Society," *Newsweek International*, November 12, 2007.

Andy Coghlan
"Autism Rises Despite MMR Ban in Japan," *New Scientist*, March 3, 2005.

Economist
"The Downturn: Greying Japan," January 7, 2006.

Blaine Harden
"Learn to Be Nice to Your Wife, or Pay the Price," *Washington Post*, November 26, 2007.

William Hollingworth
"'Institutional Racism' Lets Japan Spouses Abduct Kids," *Japan Times*, October 15, 2008.

Junko Kumamoto-Healey
"Women in the Japanese Labour Market, 1947–2003: A Brief Survey," *International Labour Review*, vol. 144, 2005.

Leo Lewis
"Japan Gripped by Suicide Epidemic," *Times Online* (London), June 19, 2008.

Toru Maegawa
"Human Rights Abuses on the Net," *Japan Spotlight*, January–February, 2008.

Norimitsu Onishi
"As Japan Ages, Prisons Adapt to Going Gray," *New York Times*, November 3, 2007.

Hideko Takayama
"Home Care: Watching Out for Mom," *Newsweek*, December 6, 2004.

What Global Role Does Japan Play?

Chapter Preface

Almost exactly halfway between South Korea and Japan lie what the United States government calls the Liancourt Rocks in the Sea of Japan. This group of islands are known as Dokdo in Korea and as Takeshima in Japan, and both nations claim them. While they are barely habitable and home to a rotating staff of Korean police and lighthouse workers, control of the islands has been the source of an ongoing dispute between the two Asian nations for more than one hundred years. Although there is significant value in natural gas deposits and a maritime base of operations, the controversy over the sovereignty of this land is partly a side effect of tensions brewing between Japan and Korea that harken back to the Japanese occupation of Korea during World War II and Japan's current attitude toward its brutal treatment of Korean civilians and soldiers.

In fact, Japan's aggressive empire-building during the first half of the twentieth century is the source of current conflict with many nations in the Pacific region. Japan's position in the world, however, has changed dramatically in the past sixty years. When Japan was ruled by an emperor, it controlled a swatch of territory that extended from the Dutch East Indies and the Philippines to as far north as land now claimed by Russia. After the war, Japan established a parliament to conduct the affairs of the nation (keeping the emperor in a largely ceremonial role), which had shrunk its territory to the original archipelago. Today it ranks only tenth on the list of the world's most populated countries, but it has the second-largest economy. It is a global leader in technological advancement and it is generally pacifist. It is a nation that has utterly transformed its global presence.

It is also a nation maintaining a tricky balancing act between reaching out to other countries and keeping to itself.

Should the wealthy and stable Japan make an effort to influence the development of the poorer nations in the region, or should it respect the wariness those nations have as former conquered states of the empire? Should Japan open its borders to immigrants to help solve the underpopulation problems that loom ahead, or should it try to preserve the unique culture and traditions that have flourished only on its islands for thousands of years? Should Japan alter its constitution to allow for a more proactive military, or will doing so trigger a direct, hostile response from the very nations Japan might need to defend itself against in the future? Should Japan protect its popular culture from outside influences or better market its culture in other countries around the globe? Japan is already the third-largest contributor of humanitarian assistance in total dollars, but it is quite far down on the list per capita—should it donate more money? To what causes?

The past several decades have been a time during which the nation of Japan could reorganize itself and take stock of its position among the nations of the world. But the world is changing again, and reflection will very soon be an insufficient tactic for addressing the major global issues—environmental, political, and medical—that lurk on the horizon. The luxury of social and political isolation that Japan has been enjoying will have to be replaced by something else. Will Japan step forward as a global leader or withdraw into its borders as a passive observer of future events?

The following chapter explores Japan's relationship with other governments and other peoples and examines how Japanese leaders and people have adapted to the changes in their country during the past half-century.

"*The Foundation of [Toyota in America]
is standardized work, meaning you fix
the rule, and you follow the rule.*"

Japanese Manufacturing Businesses Succeed Globally

Jack Smith

Jack Smith is the managing editor of Plant Engineering *magazine. He has had fifteen years experience as an engineering technician in the aviation industry. The following viewpoint focuses on a branch of the Japanese auto company Toyota that operates out of Kentucky in the United States. Smith emphasizes the "Toyota Way"—a standardized system of manufacturing—as the foundation for the company's global success.*

As you read, consider the following questions:

1. What are the two business principles of the "Toyota Way," according to Smith?
2. What does the author say are the seven types of waste identified and then eliminated from the Toyota Production System?

Jack Smith, "Driving Continuous Improvement," *Plant Engineering*, vol. 60, no. 12, December 1, 2006, p. 42. Copyright © 2006 Reed Business Information, a division of Reed Elsevier Inc. All rights reserved. Reproduced by permission.

3. What benefit does the *andon* alert system bring to the assembly line and overall manufacturing process, in Smith's view?

"We have the same equipment as our competitors," said Tom Zawacki, general manager, general administration, Toyota Motor Manufacturing, Inc., Kentucky (TMMK). "We use the same raw materials. They come from the same suppliers."

"When people come here, they ask, 'What's that silver bullet? What's that thing that makes Toyota different?'" added Rick Hesterberg, assistant manager of media relations at TMMK.

"The key is our people—they are the real key to our success, we have intelligent, flexible, highly motivated people that have a voice in what they do," Zawacki said. "Through the Continuous Improvement process we expect our team members to walk through those doors in the morning thinking 'what can I do differently today, better today, than I did yesterday,' to help make this company stronger. And that's the mindset that allows Toyota to be successful in North America and throughout the world."

And successful it is. Some of TMMK's recent achievements include:

- Produced the best selling car in America for eight out of the last nine years

- Earned 10 J.D. Power Quality Plant Awards since 1987—four of them are Gold Awards

- *Motor Trend* named the Camry its Car of the Year

- Number One Plant in North America for productivity by the *Harbour Report*

- Toyota Motor Manufacturing North America's Environmental Awards in all five areas: energy reduction, zero landfill, toxic chemical reduction, water use reduction and air emission reduction

- Kentucky Governor's Company of the Year Award

- EPA [Environmental Protection Agency] Energy Star Partner of the Year two years in a row

- *Plant Engineering's* Top Plant for 2006

The Toyota Way

The two business principles of the Toyota Way philosophy is respect for people and Continuous Improvement. The underlying tenet is simple: do the right thing for the company, its people, the customer and society as a whole. Toyota's philosophical mission is the foundation of all its other principles.

"Toyota Way is what we do every day out on the floor and the Toyota Production System [TPS] is what drives it," said John Poff, assistant manager, general assembly at TMMK, "It's the machine that's inside that makes you do what you do: standardization, Just-in-Time, Kaizen, 5s and other elements of TPS that differentiate Toyota from other manufacturers."

Toyota's philosophy can be found in every aspect of its famous Toyota Production System. Developed between 1945 and 1970, TPS is still evolving today. It is the legendary methodology that gave birth to Total Productive Maintenance and Lean Manufacturing.

Zawacki said the foundation of TPS is standardized work, meaning you fix the rule, and you follow the rule. Then you try to improve the rule with kaizen—a Japanese word for "continuous improvement."

The primary goal of TPS is to eliminate *muda*, the Japanese word for waste. TPS targets seven kinds of waste: overproduction, motion, waiting, conveyance, processing, inventory and correction—or rework.

M. Ando Reinvents the Noodle

In 2005, 86 billion servings of instant noodles were eaten around the world. . . .

In 1958 instant noodles went on the market, yellowish wormy bricks in cellophane bags, and were laughed at by fresh-noodle makers all over Japan. They were just a high-tech craze, costing six times as much as the fresh stuff; they would never catch on. . . . The Japanese voted instant noodles their most important 20th-century invention, Sony Walkmans notwithstanding. Mr Ando's firm, Nissin, became a $3 billion global enterprise.

Economist,
January 20, 2007.

The pillars that support TPS are Jidoka and Just-in-Time [JIT]. Jidoka is quality at the source. "It means we prevent defects from flowing to the next process," said Zawacki.

Training: A Top Priority

U.S. suppliers had a lot to learn about inventory, according to Zawacki. "A lot of suppliers that came to us 20 years ago when we were first establishing our supply base would say, 'We know you like JIT delivery, so we're going to have a warehouse next door, and we're going to store 30 days of inventory.' It took a long time for us to educate many of our suppliers. That's not what JIT delivery means. It means JIT manufacturing. And then you "can deliver Just-in-Time."

The Georgetown facility is set up as a Global Production Center to train its own team members as well as team members from other Toyota plants. "We have become fairly proficient manufacturers over the past 20 years," Zawacki said. "We have become the mother plant for several of the new facilities in North America."

"We actually train other facilities in TPS here," said Poff. "This teaches the team members the finer points of correct safety and methods to install parts. We train our team members, and we also have groups come here from other facilities to be trained. So we can teach them, 'this is how you put these bolts on; this is how you make this connection; this is how you set this part.'"

"We're able to help start up other Toyota plants in North America," continued Zawacki. "We helped launch the Indiana facility, the West Virginia facility, the Alabama facility, the Baja California facility. We're helping to get our joint venture with Subaru up and running, in Lafayette, [Indiana]. We are helping them develop that self-sufficiency that we have already developed ourselves."

The Toyota Way is much more than a collection of improvement and efficiency procedures. It's a culture that depends on the mindset and efforts of every team member to reduce inventory, identify problems and to eliminate waste with a sense of determination, purpose and teamwork. TPS can be imitated; the Toyota Way cannot. It must evolve over many years.

TMMK's Process

Toyota broke ground for the plant in 1986. When the first car produced there—a white Camry—rolled off the line in May of 1988, little did they know that 20 years later TMMK would be producing more than 2,000 cars a day there.

Trucks bring in coils of steel and an overhead conveyor moves them to where they are staged by dimensions, weights and gauges. From there to the finished product, "it takes a little more than 20 hours to build a Camry, Avalon or Solara," Hesterberg said.

Coiled steel gets uncoiled, washed and blanked (or cut) into different parts and stacked ready for stamping. Forklifts take them to where they are staged, ready to go to the press line.

After stamping, parts are stacked into what TMMK employees call a Minomi system: identical parts are nested and stacked, taking advantage of their shapes. Minomi minimizes wasted motion, scratches and scrap. Hesterberg said TMMK developed the Minomi system in 2004.

"Used to be, you'd see a bunch of parts crammed into a big metal rack, which is taken to the line, and team members pull them out. But now they're staged, where every part is accounted for on every car that's going to be built," he said.

A Well-Oiled Machine

Individual body parts from stamping are joined in the body weld area. Hundreds of robots do more than 90% of the car body welding. A complete car body shell emerges from body weld and is transported by conveyor to the paint shop, where it spends 9 and one-half hours.

Some companies paint multiple cars in batches before changing colors, but TMMK does not. "We're flexible enough to where if you order a red one and I order a blue one, we'll produce them in that order. We make them and paint them in the order that they come from the dealerships," said Hesterberg.

After the car body shells are painted and cured, they go to assembly. Assembly consists of chassis and final lines. Cars get engines in the chassis area, a process that people at TMMK, call "engine marriage." "We use a hydraulic lift to bring the engine from underneath the car, as opposed to hoisting them overhead," Hesterberg said. "It's a lot less stress on the engine; less stress on the workers; and it's a better fit—more consistency."

Engines are manufactured onsite in a facility next door to the main assembly plants—Plant 1 and Plant 2. "We also have an engine plant in Buffalo, [West Virginia]. They [also] do our transmissions," explained Hesterberg.

With the equivalent of 156 football fields under one roof, assembly is by far the largest area in the plant. Cars advance up one line and down another. Although there appear to be multiple parallel production lines, a vehicle transfer mechanism and a buffer, which holds six to nine car bodies, connect each one, making one continuous production line with well-thought-out sections.

Assembly Never Stops

Andon cords hang overhead on both sides of each line section. When a team member sees a problem, he or she pulls the cord. *Andon* means "little sign." But here, pulling the andon cord causes a light to flash, an annunciator to illuminate and a cheerful song to play—scales, triads or even a song from Beethoven. Andon alerts the team leader that a team member has found a problem. Rather than pass that problem on to the next process in the line, or eventually to the customer, the team member, team leader or both have a certain amount of time to correct the problem before the line actually stops. Most of the time, problems are resolved before a line stop occurs. But if it does stop, the transfer buffers at the end of each line section keep processes downstream moving. An andon cord gets pulled every few minutes somewhere in the factory. Jidoka prevents these problems from flowing to the next process.

"We monitor the facility through our information portals," Poff said. "By looking at andon reporting systems I can tell how each line is running. I can understand how much downtime they've had; I can understand where their actual issues are. If I click on the information portal for Trim 1, it will show me process-by-process—based on the andon number—what the actual condition is in real time.

"We can look at hourly status; I can look at current defect level. If there is a problem, I can go into any of the kiosks, type in a message and tell the management team above me exactly what's wrong in real time."

The "just enough" mindset extends to TMMK's application of automation. "When people talk about automation, a lot of folks have the wrong impression," Zawacki said. "A lot of folks think that a state-of-the-art plant means it is highly automated. That may be true at some manufacturers, but we don't automate for the sake of automation. We automate when a job is not safe; when the job requires greater precision; or it can be done at a higher level of quality than a human hand could do it—when it makes sense to for the productivity of the job."

> "The Japanese have a poorly developed sense of how to profit from their creative output—especially when it comes to intellectual property."

Japanese Entertainment Businesses Suffer Globally

Roland Kelts

Roland Kelts is a writer of fiction and nonfiction, an editor of a literary journal, and a lecturer at the University of Tokyo. His work has appeared in a variety of publications, from the fashion magazine Vogue *to the special collection* Gamers. *He divides his time between Japan and New York. In the following viewpoint Kelts argues that although animation styles and characters are recognized and emulated worldwide, Japanese designers of these art and cultural products do not make large profits from licensing and merchandising.*

As you read, consider the following questions:

1. What is the most likely explanation for why Japanese business models are not fully tapping the global anime market, in Kelts's opinion?

2. What factors, in the author's view are contributing to the problems of attracting and keeping talent in the animation industry?

3. How might increased funding and commercial success affect anime as an art form, according to Kelts?

Excepting their successes in the automotive and electronics industries, the Japanese have a poorly developed sense of how to profit from their creative output—especially when it comes to intellectual property. The industry that postwar giants [Osamu] Tezuka and [Hayao] Miyazaki pioneered is, domestically at least, pretty thin on the ground.

"We had a similar problem in the U.S. between 1955 and 1975," says critic [Charles] Solomon. "The old studios were closing down, and for some reason Disney didn't hire anyone new. The same artists from *Show White* would make *101 Dalmatians* in the '60s. And this country suffered from a gap where almost everyone in animation was over 65 or under 35. Teachers were lost. A whole generation didn't receive the education.

"I just hope the Japanese learn from us," he adds, "and make an industry that pays more attractively." . . .

Animation Globally Popular

As Shinichiro Ishikawa, the president and founder of animation studio Gonzo Digimation Holdings (GDH) notes: "Japan has no lack of creativity—that is not the problem. We have the creative wheel, but we lack the capital wheel. So our cart just spins round and round." From a simple glance at the numbers, this should be the dawning of a golden age for Japanese animation. All but one of Japan's listed animation companies were profitable [in 2005] and others are preparing for their IPOs [initial public offering of stock].

Without any really serious marketing strategies of their own devising, over the past five years Japanese animation studios have nurtured a fast-rising fan base in the United States and rekindled the old passions of European fans of the genre. Feature films like *Spirited Away* and *Howl's Moving Castle* have made their mark in cinemas from Rome to Reno. The Cartoon Network fills about half its airtime with Japanese or mock-Japanese animations; the Akira Kurosawa-inspired *Samurai 7* is a weekly feature on the U.S.-based Independent Film Channel; . . . *Afro Samurai* is set to debut on Spike TV with a feature film to follow.

The domestic Japanese market is even hotter. [In 2002] Japanese TV was broadcasting fifty new anime titles every week; [in 2006] they are broadcasting eighty. Satellite channels at home and abroad mean that most Japanese animators have around five hits from their back catalog being reaired at any given time. In a land where the art form is now at least forty years old, inventory is everything.

Tremendous Marketing Potential

The scope of product tie-ins—from video games to cuddly toys—is potentially enormous. Japanese animators have long had the knack for making their storylines an addictive mix of never-ending plot twists. *Dragonball* has been going for twenty years, and the saga shows no signs of drawing to a close. A third generation of seven-year-olds is primed to get hooked.

And technology has opened extraordinary new ways to sell and resell animation. The form has found an ideal home on the screens of third-generation mobile phones, and the anime industry is shaping up as the first to introduce video-on-demand Internet services properly—something that has for many years been sought as the Holy Grail of the media future.

But just scratch the surface a bit, and suddenly the scene is anything but blissful. The global anime boom of the twenty-first century has taken Japan, a country whose corporate culture prides itself on knowing the next new thing, almost completely by surprise.

The people who should have their fingers firmly affixed to the pulse of western pop culture passions are groping around in the dark. Executives of major animation studios have declared that they do not think Gundam is popular outside Japan, and that robots are probably too Japanese to appeal to foreign tastes. They are staggered when a foreigner reels off names like Cowboy Bebop or North Star Ken with familiar ease. And if you come up with something slightly out of the mainstream, like Jin-Roh, they declare you an *otaku* [a Japanese term to refer to people who have obsessive interests, particularly anime, manga, and video games] obsessive.

The Business Blind Spot

Every animation professional and/or guru has his or her own explanation for the industry-wide blind spot. The most convincing is that the global interest in animation is not driven by any forces that the industry either recognizes or knows how to exploit. For domestic growth, animators in Japan used to rely on the so-called golden triangle of anime, toys, and video games—a structure of Japanese origin that meant that at any given time you needed popularity of only two out of the three to create and whip up a market for the third. It was effective and predictable and, above all, controllable.

But in the case of the United States in particular, the Internet is playing a colossal role in generating the buzz for and around anime. For Japanese animators, this is new, unknown, and untamable territory, and their response to it has been poor to pathetic. Rather than embracing the fact that there is a new generation of animation geeks cropping up everywhere, and peddling to their every desire, Japan has on this occasion let America dictate its terms.

As a senior board member of Toei Animation remarks with a baffled grin: "It amazes me. For the past two years we have had overseas buyers here all the time! These foreign buyers have so much information about which animes have been popular in Japan, and these are the ones they go for. I have no idea how they accumulate all this information."

Anime presents Japan with a business conundrum that it has never directly experienced in the past, and one for which there is nobody to offer reliable guidance. Japanese industries that have made their names selling abroad have traditionally been manufacturing-based, such as the automotive and electronics industries, and have watched over their products with a neurotic obsessive-compulsiveness. They have crafted the market to suit their exacting needs—and thrown tantrums or imploded completely when the markets shift away from their model. Clearly, they have not provided the anime industry with the help it needs. . . .

Learning to Appreciate Anime

Ishikawa of GDH is . . . a hard-nosed entrepreneur with a sophisticated understanding of where the international market is heading and the future value of anime as intellectual property. Japan has a social infrastructure—unique in the world—where people of all ages and backgrounds read manga comics. The range of subjects covered in pictorial form is therefore vast and, as anime becomes more popular, gives Japan an edge over the rest of the world that it could retain for decades.

Ishikawa founded his company [in 2000] on the theory that, in a broadband digital world, animation would be king. He has embraced the international potential of anime, rather than treating it as a surprise bonus.

He believes that the trouble with the industry lies in the Japanese mindset and the dominance of what he calls "emotional money" over "professional money." Professionals, he says, care about returns, and that is what Japan is missing. The troubled times for anime—just when it should be blossoming into a global money-spinner—encapsulate problems that affect not just the corporate world but the whole of Japanese society. Japan, he argues, has a problem comprehending

The Most Successful Anime and Animation Films in the Box Office

Anime

Rank	Title	Lifetime gross in U.S. dollars
1	*Pokemon: The First Movie*	$85,744,662
2	*Pokemon: The Movie 2000*	$43,758,684
3	*Yu-Gi-Oh! The Movie*	$19,765,868
4	*Pokemon 3: The Movie*	$17,052,128
5	*Spirited Away*	$10,055,859

Animation

Rank	Title	Lifetime gross in U.S. dollars
1	*Shrek 2*	$441,226,247
2	*Finding Nemo*	$339,714,978
3	*The Lion King*	$328,541,776
4	*Shrek the Third*	$322,719,944
5	*Shrek*	$267,665,011

TAKEN FROM: "Animation—Anime" and "Animation 1980–Present," Box Office Mojo, 2007. www.boxofficemojo.com.

the very idea of intellectual property, and anime represents the first time that the country has really faced the possibility that it may one day be better at exporting ideas than cars and DVD players.

Japan, he explains, is intrinsically scared of investing in the media industry because it is not perceived to be "real." He believes that anime needs to inflate a financial bubble, where investors come to believe in the future worth of intangibles.

"I was at NHK [Japan Broadcasting Corporation] and one of the people there said, 'Don't you think it is crazy that actors in Hollywood get $20 million for a film? We should not get into that in Japan.' I told him that that is exactly what's wrong with Japanese thinking. What we so badly need is an investment bubble for anime." . . .

Adapting to Foreign Markets

Meanwhile, for the "old" side of the industry, the western anime boom is causing a variety of headaches, but also offering clues for a solution to deeper problems that anime studios have long faced. Katsuhiro Yamada, the chief financial officer of TMS [Entertainment]—the company behind *Anpanman, Ulysees 31*, and dozens of other classics—is initially negative about the prospects of big foreign growth. His company has no serious presence in the United States and is desperately looking for people to staff its lone Los Angeles office.

"To be honest, we have not worked out what is the best content for the foreign market. I admit that we have not made the utmost effort to get into the overseas market, so now we are doing everything we can to catch up. If we get a demand for ten anime, I think we can do seven or eight, but there is a lack of communication between what they want and what we can provide. I suppose . . . we are in a kind of panic."

As he continues, the story of an industry in the throes of dramatic transformation fast unfolds. Is it possible that the industry's problems with exploiting the U.S. and European anime booms are not terminal, but merely the symptoms of a patient coming out of a long coma? Could it be that the Japanese animation industry is not riddled with incompetence and inflexibility, but is quietly biding its time and changing its form to become as formidable abroad as it is in its domestic market?

Yamada describes the very recent phenomenon of the "Anime Consortium"—an ad hoc collection of producers and investors who raise the capital needed to make whatever is demanded by the market. In existence for about nine years, it is quietly establishing itself as the best way of financing animation. Handled right, the model will give anime companies the previously unattainable ability to say "yes" to any type of request that rolls in from abroad. If NBC [National Broadcasting Company] wants thirty new episodes of *North Star*

Ken, TMS and everyone else in the consortium will not be forced to turn the U.S. buyers away.

Mitsunobu Seiji, president of Studio Hibari, claims that the answer lies in the formation of a union capable of collectively securing favorable deals in the international market. He points to the relatively small U.S. profits made by Nintendo, despite the spectacular overseas success of its Pokémon title. By settling for a flat fee upfront and ignoring royalties, Nintendo, despite its size and apparent savvy, made far less out of the phenomenon than 4Kids, its U.S. distributor. "The animators need to protect themselves and make a change to the system," says Seiji. "We need a union." . . .

Popularity Threatens Quality

Japanese anime's popularity in the West now threatens the very source of the quality that makes it so attractive. The new demand has caused a dangerous hollowing out of talent in Japan. "The new generation are 'kamikaze animators,'" says Okao, "who are only taught how to take off and fly straight. Before they have time to become great, they burn out. When I was young, we had three years of training. Now, if you are an in-betweener for more than half a year, people say your career has stalled. There are just too many projects going on at the same time."

Further exacerbating the hollowing out of Japanese talent is increasing competition from Japan's Asian neighbors. Many major studios are quietly outsourcing the more laborious aspects of the production process—especially the in-betweener work, in which aspiring artists painstakingly fill in the cel-by-cel movements that take you from scene to scene. Indeed, Tezuka Productions proudly features its' Beijing facility in its corporate brochures and on its Web site.

Lower-cost facilities and labor provided by the Koreans, the Chinese, and Southeast Asians can mean a much wider profit margin, of course, but also far fewer opportunities for work, and cash, for hopeful young Japanese anime artists. . . .

"Nowadays the young ones want a decent income and time to enjoy their lives," concedes Matsuhisa Ishikawa of Production IG, the makers of *Ghost in the Shell*, a seminal work in anime's success in the West. "And it's not a good idea for us to identify this as a poor industry. People will not join."

2dk's [David] d'Heilly is less sparing in his analysis. "When something works abroad, [Japan's animators] don't see a nickel of it. And most of the producers have done a pretty shoddy job of protecting their industry. And now, here come the Taiwanese, here come the Vietnamese. And the Japanese can feel it all going away from them, just slipping away." . . .

Cultural Differences

[Satoshi] Ito, the elderly Mushi president, and a friend and former colleague of Tezuka, sits down with me to explain why his industry needs help. He has run the crumbling anime studio since being handpicked by Tezuka in the 1970s.

Like everyone else who has spent time with Tezuka, Ito toes the official line when talking about Disney. He holds forth on the anime industry beneath framed, yellowing pictures of Astro Boy and Kimba the Lion. But he also has the glint in his eye—that fleeting shimmer, visible in so many corners of Japanese industry, and seeming to say: "We have to respect you, but we do this stuff better than you."

He is quick to point out that even when countries in Europe, particularly France, were nervously putting official limits on the amount of Japanese animation that could be shown on TV, their own domestic animators were quietly outsourcing all their production to Japan.

"What makes Japanese animation different? In the U.S., you [need] a person to act out a movement then draw what you see. Japan doesn't need all that. Our animators can just imagine the movement in their heads," he says. "I am frankly surprised that the country that produced Disney is interested at all in Japanese anime. Can they truly appreciate what we do?"

But even Ito has to admit that when it comes to funding the future of anime, Japan may turn to the United States for its model. He believes that the fledgling use of anime funds and consortia . . . will continue to grow. He wonders aloud whether that will ultimately be good for the industry, leaving little doubt where he stands.

"People who invest in animation will want a return. The concern I have is that only anime that will definitely be major hits will actually get made. There will be no diversity. This particular film I'm working on is too low budget to be worth forming a fund for. But popular themes will be the ones where millions can be made from tie-ins with manga, toys, or video games. They will dominate in a fund-backed-only environment. Nobody will take on the difficult themes any more." . . .

The Legacy of Anime

But the real revelation is yet to come. Ito shuffles ahead of me, guiding me down another musty, narrow corridor, from which doors lead off to small animation sweatshops. He opens the door to a dust-floored back room and hastily shoves cardboard boxes and other clutter aside. He snaps on a light to illuminate a matte black piece of aging machinery—a machine that allowed a film camera to be mounted above the animation cels as they were hand-wound in front of the lens.

"This was the machine that Tezuka made *Astro Boy* with," says Ito, his eyes squinting with sad pride. "We tried to give it to a museum, but nobody wanted it."

The Japanese animation industry, after fifty years of commercial and artistic success, and despite its role as perhaps Japan's most important cultural export of the last thirty, has not gained "establishment" status. Its products are iconic nearly everywhere, a few of its creators are lauded as superstars, but the symbolic piece of its inception is an irrelevance—a rusting machine in a dusty room. If the film camera on which *Gone with the Wind* had been up for grabs, it seems likely some collector would bid thousands of dollars, if not much more, to own it.

Japanese collectors are willing and prepared to pay high prices to own remnants of their beloved pop culture. According to analyses by the Nomura Research Institute, they spend around $4 billion annually, a fact that Japanese corporations recognized forty years ago, exploited domestically, and then, as they do with nearly every other native creation, exported.

But with anime and manga in particular, it seems that so much emphasis was placed upon producing the art that the industry forgot, or was simply too single-minded, to get the word out to potential investors. Now it is being forced to.

"At the close of World War II, . . . whale meat provided a lifeline to a truly starving population, . . . earning itself a revered position in the nation's food culture."

Japan Has a Right to Preserve Its Whaling Heritage

Colin Woodard

Colin Woodard is a journalist and the author of several nonfiction books. A recipient of the Pew Fellowship in International Journalism, he has covered many global environment topics, from the destruction of coral reefs to global warming. In 1986, the International Whaling Commission placed a moratorium on whale hunting; Japan is one of only a few nations still practicing commercial whaling. In the following viewpoint, Woodard places Japanese whale hunting in a historical context and argues that the Japanese people have justification for continuing an industry that is globally controversial to the point of vilification.

As you read, consider the following questions:

1. If commercial whaling has been banned in Japan, where does Woodard say the whales being used for food are coming from?

2. How has Japan garnered support from other nations for its whaling industry, according to the author?

3. According to the spokesperson for Tokyo's Institute for Cetacean Research, as cited by Woodard, why do people object to whale meat but not the meat of other animals?

If you're into eating whales, Kouji Shingru's shop is the place for you.

Located on a pedestrian-only street in Tokyo's bustling Asakusa neighborhood, Shingru's compact establishment has it all: deep red whale steaks and fillets in vacuum-sealed packages, cured whale on a stick, snack-sized bags of whale jerky, and a wide selection of canned whale morsels packed in brown sauce. A steady stream of customers—most of them over 50— flows through the Yushi Special Shop in Whales, one of the capital's only retail outlets for whale products.

"Almost all those who like whale meat are middle-aged and older," says Shingru, a middle-aged man himself. "Young people have no experience with eating whale. In fact, my shop is one of the only places where young people have a chance to eat it."

Whaling Ban Limits Supply

The problem, says Shingru, is with the supply. Since 1986, commercial whaling has been banned by the International Whaling Commission [IWC] and whale-eating nations have had to make do with the byproducts of their scientific catch. Japan—whose people once killed and ate thousands of blue, fin, sperm, sei, and humpback whales in a single season—has in recent years subsisted on an annual supply of 500 to 600 minke whales, each only a third the size of the fin whales that were once the backbone of the country's whaling industry.

"Twenty years ago there was a lot of whale meat, and whale was a popular fish," Shingru explains. "Now there is very little available, and whale meat is very expensive." He holds up a 100-gram package of fresh minke bacon, white and light pink in color, selling for 1,800 yen ($15.30)—too dear for many consumers, he says. "Twenty years ago, this would have cost one-tenth as much."

That may be about to change. [In 2006] Japan has more than doubled its whaling quota to 935 minkes, ostensibly as part of long-term research into the size and health of their population in the frigid waters around Antarctica. Norway has also boosted its quota in the North Atlantic, upsetting anti-whaling activists who note that [2006] will be the world's most deadly whaling season in a generation.

Indeed, 2006 could well be the year that the international whaling moratorium collapses altogether. In a triumph of patient diplomacy, Japan has used aid and trade measures to convince a small army of previously disinterested Caribbean and Pacific nations to join the IWC and vote with Japan. When the IWC meets in St. Kitts in the Caribbean, the pro-whaling bloc may well have the votes to overturn the ban. [They did.] Whale, it seems, is back on the menu.

The Case for Whaling

Many in the West see a resumption of whaling as barbaric, a return to the dark days of the 20th century, when floating factories drove many great whales to the brink of extinction to procure industrial oil and pet food. But people in whale-eating nations see the issue differently, and find some of the criticisms by other countries hypocritical.

In Norway, even leading environmental groups like the Oslo-based Bellona Foundation support the country's whale hunt. "We use small fishing vessels that consume few inputs and cause almost no pollution—it's very friendly eco-production," says Bellona's Marius Holm. "Our principle is that we should harvest what nature provides, but in a sustainable way regarding the ecosystem as a whole and the specific stocks." As long as it's done sustainably, he adds, "We think whaling is a good thing."

Using those criteria, it's hard to disagree. Norway's government-sanctioned hunt is controversial—it's the only country in the world that has a commercial hunt in defiance of the moratorium—but it does appear to be sustainable. Operating from about 30 small fishing vessels, Norway's whalers are allowed to kill up to 1,052 minkes out of a total estimated North Atlantic population of roughly 100,000. "The hunt we have had along our coast has always been sustainable," says Halvard Johansen of the Norwegian Ministry of Fisheries. "We've been whaling on this coast since the ninth century, and we don't see that big a difference between aboriginal whaling and what we do here." (Native residents in Alaska, Canada, Greenland, and St. Vincent and the Grenadines are permitted a limited annual subsistence hunt.)

"We utilize the whole animal—nothing is thrown away," Icelandic whaler Kristjan Loftsson told me when I visited his country. Loftsson is managing director of Iceland's four-boat whaling fleet, which catches about 40 minkes each year under a science permit. "We feel that we're being hung for mistakes made 80 years ago in the Antarctic."

Our interview started on the deck of one of Loftsson's 150-foot steam-powered boats, which are so small they return from a hunt with one or two minke carcasses strapped to the outside of the hull. (The animals are butchered on shore.) But when my questions turned to the whale's place in Icelandic food culture, Loftsson insisted we adjourn to 3 Frakkar, a nearby Reykjavik restaurant whose deep freezers have kept its tables supplied with whale throughout the moratorium.

Whale Meat: A Healthy Alternative?

	Whale (4 oz beluga)	Beef (4 oz lean sirloin)	Chicken (4 oz skinless breast)	Salmon (4 oz farmed)
Calories Total	124	160	124	204
Fats (g)	0	8	0	12
Protein (g)	28	24	24	24
Cholesterol (mg)	88	48	64	68
Sodium (mg)	88	60	72	68
Key Vitamins & Minerals	zinc, niacin, B12, iron, phosphorus, selenium	B12, phosphorus, zinc, niacin, B6, selenium	phosphorus, niacin, B6, selenium	thiamin, B6, phosphorus, niacin, B12, selenium

TAKEN FROM: Nutrition Data: Know What You Eat, November 10, 2008. www.nutritiondata.com.

The fin whale is served as sashimi, and looks and tastes like a cross between high-grade tuna and beef tenderloin. Despite spending 20 years in 3 Frakkar's freezers, it's subtle and delicious. "It's the best sushi meat you can have," Loftsson proclaims, his beard shaking with enthusiasm, "but here we eat it mostly as grilled meat."

When the small dish is finished, I have some misgivings about having eaten part of a great whale, but the experience can't fail to impress just how many meals a single whale must produce. In terms of food per life taken, it's hard to compete with an 80-ton mammal—that's 35,000 times the live weight of a chicken.

The Cultural Struggle

In Tokyo, Shingru had a back room where customers could eat their whale purchases, but I settled for a portable bag of minke whale jerky. It tasted something like beef jerky, only sweeter, as promised by the text on the package: "This Kuzira Jerky tastes sweet," it read in English, "one's dear old taste."

The last reference was targeted at older Japanese who lived through the famine years at the close of World War II. In those days, whale meat provided a lifeline to a truly starving population, accounting for nearly half of all animal protein consumption, and earning itself a revered position in the nation's food culture. "It is no exaggeration to say that the blood of the whale has flow[ed] in each Japanese person who has consumed whale as [an] important gift from the sea," wrote Takeo Koizumi of the Tokyo University of Agriculture in a whaling association newsletter in 2003.

But a generation gap exists, says Hideki Moronuki, chief of the division that oversees whaling at the Japanese Fisheries Agency. "Whale meat is more than twice as expensive as yellowfin tuna, and many people, particularly the younger generation, can't afford it," he notes. "The quantity of whale meat provided by the market has increased because of the expansion of our research"—the meat from the additional whales captured for science must not be wasted, under IWC rules— "but still the price is not cheap."

If the IWC moratorium is lifted, prices could go down— but demand, not supply, may become Japan's problem. Even with an expanded scientific hunt, hundreds of tons of unsold whale meat have been piling up in storage freezers.

Now there's even a campaign to introduce whale to Japanese children and teens. Schools in Wakayama, a whaling region, have added the meat to their lunch program. "Whale culture" lessons have been added to elementary-school curricula, and one fast-food chain has started serving whale burgers, to a storm of international criticism.

But Glenn Inwood, a New Zealander who serves as spokesperson for Tokyo's Institute for Cetacean Research, thinks the anti-whaling argument has become philosophical, not scientific. "It has really come down to whether or not you think the whale resource should be used at all, regardless of their abundance," he says. Opposition, he says, is fueled by public revulsion over harpooning and flensing—the process of removing blubber from the carcass—two practices that opponents have videotaped for distribution.

In the end, supporters say the whale hunt is not all that different from the mainstream meat industry. "Many of us live in cities and eat meat wrapped in plastic and manage to have our eyes closed to where it came from," Inwood says. "The one thing the meat industry has been successful at is making sure nobody sees what happens inside a slaughterhouse."

> "In 1975, only 1.7 percent of the total daily intake of animal protein per capita came from whale meat and since the 1980s the share has been almost zero."

Japan Has No Whaling Heritage to Preserve

Atsushi Ishii and Ayako Okubo

Atsushi Ishii is an associate professor and political scientist at Tohoku University in Miyagi, Japan. Ayako Okubo is a research fellow at the Ocean Policy Research Foundation (a private institution) in Tokyo, Japan. Both authors are opponents of Japan's whaling industry, an industry that its critics claim cannot be scientifically or culturally justified. Japan does not abide by a global moratorium on the hunting and killing of whales for scientific and commercial purposes, and it justifies its position, in part, by claiming a long tradition of whaling. In the following viewpoint, the authors examine and contest that claim.

Atsushi Ishii and Ayako Okubo, "An Alternative Explanation of Japan's Whaling Diplomacy in the Post-Moratorium Era," *Journal of International Wildlife Law and Policy*, Vol. 10, January–March 2007, pp. 55–87. Copyright © 2007 by Taylor & Francis Group, LLC. Reproduced by permission of Taylor & Francis, Ltd., http://www.tandf.co.uk journals and the author.

As you read, consider the following questions:

1. For what three reasons did Japan originally protest the proposed moratorium on whale hunting in the early 1970s, according to the authors?

2. When did references to whale meat as a source of dietary protein and whaling as a cultural activity first start to appear in journalistic and government texts, according to Ishii and Okubo?

3. If the Japanese people do not generally eat whale meat, why do so many of them support Japan's continued hunting of whales, in the authors' opinion?

The International Whaling Commission (IWC) has been one of the few negotiation arenas where Japan is at the center of world attention. Japan is the only major whaling nation that must negotiate with the anti-whaling nations to lift the 1982 moratorium before resuming commercial whaling under the auspices of the International Convention for the Regulation of Whaling (ICRW). Japan's whaling diplomacy has thus attracted the attention of not only the IWC participants but also numerous scholars who are struggling to explain the underlying reasons for Japan's behavior in the IWC and its rejection of the anti-whaling norm. . . .

Japan and the IWC Process

There is no need here to repeat the history of the IWC which has swung between two extremes: from the tragic failure of not conserving cetaceans to the transformation of IWC into a preservationist regime. Japan, one of the leading actors of the entire IWC narrative, is always given the role of a defeated country or a victim of the prevailing preservationism. However, our argument fundamentally questions this way of depicting IWC history, after the negotiation phase to lift the moratorium began in around 1991. So, focusing on this phase, we here provide a brief overview of the history of Japanese whaling diplomacy relevant to the testing of our argument.

In the preparation for the 1972 United Nations Conference on the Human Environment (UNCHE), the moratorium proposal included in the Secretariat's draft action plan was unexpected for Japan because it had never been discussed in the Preparatory Committees. The Japanese Government cited three reasons why it was against the proposal: firstly, whale meat was a major source of protein for the Japanese people; secondly, the IWC had already protected all endangered species; and thirdly, the proposal was not based on sound science. The third reason is an example of the scientism that is persistently used by the Japanese Government, even today. In the exchange of views between Japan and the United States regarding the UNCHE, the then director general of the Environment Agency (the current Ministry of Environment), Buichi Ōishi, expressed his views in an official letter that Japan would support the moratorium of whaling in the future. This was soon rebutted by Ministry of Foreign Affairs (MOFA) and FA [Fisheries Agency] officials, who said that Ōishi's view was only a personal reflection and that they could not support it. The whole issue of whaling falls under the jurisdiction of the FA (with few exceptions), and the Environment Ministry has no voice in whaling issues.

In the aftermath of the UNCHE, it was clear that because of the global dismantling of the whaling industry, the moratorium campaign was increasingly becoming one of the "least cost options" for most countries to address growing public concern about the increasing derogation of the environment. Japan, for its part, had few countermeasures but to base its opposition to the moratorium on the exact legal texts of the ICRW (the "moratorium is against the objective of the ICRW"), scientism (the "moratorium is not based on sound science"), and culturalization of the whaling issue ("whale

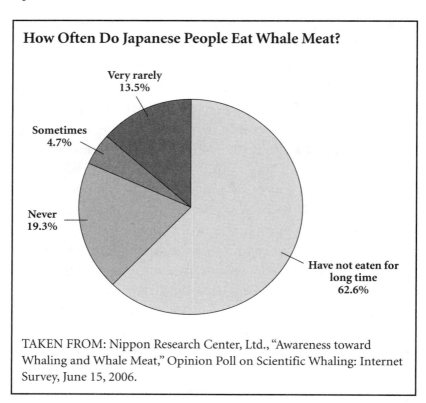

How Often Do Japanese People Eat Whale Meat?

Very rarely
13.5%

Sometimes
4.7%

Never
19.3%

Have not eaten for
long time
62.6%

TAKEN FROM: Nippon Research Center, Ltd., "Awareness toward Whaling and Whale Meat," Opinion Poll on Scientific Whaling: Internet Survey, June 15, 2006.

meat is part of Japanese dietary culture"). These remain the basis of Japan's arguments against the moratorium. . . .

A Recent Argument

We are not saying that there is no genuine traditional whaling culture in Japan. We are certainly aware of the well documented Japanese whaling culture especially in the four rural areas: Abashiri, Ayukawa, Taiji, and Wadaura. What we argue is that cultural arguments as a rhetorical strategy in the whaling debate is a recent construct. For example, despite the fact that Japanese whaling, concentrated in those four regions, flourished before World War II, the word "culture" in the whaling-related context did appear in neither *the Asahi Shimbun* (one of Japan's oldest and largest daily newspapers), nor in the minutes of the Japanese Diet [legislature] *until the late*

1970s. If Japanese whaling culture was a major explanatory factor in the Japanese refusal of the global norm, there would have to be some reference to the word *bunka* [culture] in either the mass media or the Diet at least from 1972, when the global moratorium was unexpectedly adopted by the UNCHE. We now turn to the question of how the whaling camp has pursued this "whaling as culture" strategy.

As mentioned above, the Japanese government initially used the "whales as a major source of protein" discourse to refute the moratorium proposal discussed in the UNCHE. Such a strategy gives the perception that whale meat is a basic human need for Japan, which was no more true at that time than it is today. Thereafter, the Japanese policymakers gradually increased the use of the "whaling as dietary culture" discourse in reaction to the growing moratorium controversy, and finally the discourse was incorporated into the official position of the Japanese Government. The usage of the word *tampakushitsu* [protein] (or *tampakugen* [protein source]) was substituted by *bunka* [culture] from 1979 in the Diet and *the Asahi Shimbun*, and that the usage of *bunka* peaked several times in response to major victories by the anti-whaling movement and around the time of the two IWC annual meetings in Japan (Kyoto, 1993 and Shimonoseki, 2002). Since 1987, the two main components of the Japanese Government's discourse are this nation-wide dietary culture which we concentrate on hereafter, and local culture in the aforementioned four rural areas.

The discourse dissemination strategy began in the aftermath of the UNCHE, when the JWA [Japanese Whaling Association] entrusted a private advertising corporate agency (Kokusai PR) with its public relations campaign. The strategy for the domestic campaign was twofold. By the early 1970s, the editorial writers of major Japanese newspapers, which are the most powerful influence on the public and policy agenda, gave only moderate support to continuing whaling. Therefore, the first strategy was to change their opinions. This was done by telling the writers that the anti-whaling campaign was a US conspiracy to divert the world's attention from its ocean dumping of nuclear waste. The report of the Kokusai PR itself evaluates this strategy as successful by noting the changing tone of the editorial comments of the newspapers to a more favorable one from their perspective. This success apparently laid the ground for the popularization of the "whaling as dietary culture" discourse among the Japanese public, despite the fact that nationwide whale-eating had only a short history. The second strategy, which was also successful according to Kokusai PR, was to organize a group of opinion leaders sympathetic to promoting whaling. This group, called the "Hogei Mondai Kondankai" [forum on whaling issues], played an important role in disseminating the cultural discourse. For example, the report of the group's public appeal, announced in 1979, marked the first appearance of the word *bunka* [culture] in *the Asahi Shimbun* in a whaling-related context.

Culture Clash

While these activities by JWA were not part of the official policymaking process, the official promotion of the cultural discourse was first made in 1984 by the aforementioned Hogei Mondai Kentōkai [investigation panel on whaling issues]. Since the 1980s, the cultural discourse has appeared constantly in official remarks by Japanese policymakers and documents, and takes the form of characterizing the moratorium controversy as a "clash of meat-eating and fish-eating (whale-eating) cultures" or "cultural imperialism" by the Western countries. But the dietary culture discourse cannot be validated against reality. Even in 1975, only 1.7 percent of the total daily intake of animal protein per capita came from whale meat and since the 1980s the share has been almost zero. It was reported in 2001 that all available whale meat, mainly from research whaling, could not sell out in the Japanese market for the first time.

Public opinion polls show that many Japanese citizens support the basic stance of the Japanese Government: dietary culture should be mutually respected. But this is not because they want to eat whale meat, indicating that their support has been won thanks to the framing of the moratorium controversy as a debate about cultural imperialism, and that their opposition to the anti-whaling movement is heavily salted with nationalism.

Periodical Bibliography

Karlyn Bowman — "Data Points: How Japan Sees Itself, the U.S., and the World," *American*, July–August 2007.

Steven Clayson — "Sino-Japanese Oil Controversy Underscores Global Tensions," *ResourceInvestor.com*, April 18, 2005. www.resourceinvestor.com.

Martin Fackler — "Japan Leader's First Bow Is to Asian Neighbors," *New York Times*, October 4, 2006.

Richard Halloran — "Japan Sliding," *Washington Times*, November 5, 2008.

Gao Hong — "Prejudices Make Most Japanese Wary of China," *China Daily*, September 1, 2008. www.chinadaily.com.cn.

Timur Khursandov — "No Breakthrough in Peace Treaty Talks," *Kommersant (Russia)*, November 5, 2008. www.kommersant.com.

Seyoon Kim — "South Korea, Japan Discuss Ways to Stabilize Markets," *Bloomberg News*, November 6, 2008. www.bloomberg,com.

Justin McCurry — "Big Sushi: The World's Most Politically Sensitive Lunch," *Monthly: Australian Politics, Society, & Culture*, August 2006.

B. Raman — "India & Japan: Impact of Relationship on China," *Global News Blog*, August 22, 2007. globalnewsblog.com.

Adario Strange — "Google/YouTube Slammed by Japanese Coalition," *Wired*, August 2, 2007. www.blog.wired.com.

Shaun Tandon — "Greenpeace Says It Will Not Chase Japanese Whalers," *Agence France-Presse*, November 4, 2008.

Sayuri Umeda — "Controversy over Payment for U.S. Military Bases," *Global Legal Monitor*, June 2, 2008.

OPPOSING
VIEWPOINTS®
SERIES

CHAPTER 3

How Does Modern Living Conflict with Tradition in Japan?

Chapter Preface

According to the *CIA World Factbook*, nearly 99 percent of the people of Japan are ethnically and racially Japanese. Compare that with the population of the United States, where, according to the *World Factbook*, the largest ethnic/racial group—white people—comprises 80 percent of the population (a figure that includes many people of Hispanic/Latino descent, a group that makes up an estimated 15 percent of the population). Another large ethnic/racial group—African Americans—comprises nearly 13 percent, with the remaining population representing a multitude of ethnic and racial backgrounds. The official language of Japan is Japanese, and 99 percent of the population speaks it. The official language of the United States is English, but only 80 percent of the people speak it. U.S. government documents, including voter registration materials, are provided in Spanish for the 10 percent of the people who speak that language and, depending on the state or city you live in, you might see forms and other materials written in Tagalog or Vietnamese, too. Other nations in the world are even more diverse than the United States, but compared with the United States, the ethnic and racial homogeneity of Japan seems complete. For some Japanese people, living in the midst of a homogeneous society sparks an urge to differentiate themselves, an urge that may be expressed through fashion.

Japan is famous for its costume play, known as "cosplay" around the world and as *reyazu* in Japan (a variation on the English word, "players"). Although most Japanese people do not engage in cosplay, the ones who do stand out brightly in a crowd. The costumes that players wear are elaborate ensembles copied from or inspired by characters from animated films and programs, and manga (graphic novels and stories). Participants can spend months designing and making their costumes or buy premade costumes in stores. Some people go so far as to rigorously diet and exercise in order to achieve the lean lines or physical strength that their adopted characters possess. Reyazu appear at comic markets and conventions (just like people in the United States will dress up for science fiction events), but they also gather on the streets in shopping districts and elsewhere to show off their looks and to reenact scenes with other characters in displays of performance art.

There are subcultures among the cosplayers, too. Consider, for example, the Lolitas: they are girls who dress in Victorian clothing to resemble as closely as possible porcelain dolls. They wear bonnets, crinolines, and bodices, and carry parasols in the style of English fashions from the nineteenth century. Even within the Lolita culture are subgroups: "Sweet" Lolitas, "Goth" Lolitas, "Punk" Lolitas, and "Classic" Lolitas, as well as adaptations of male clothing from the same period. But not all costumes are inspired by fantasy or history. The hallmark of the "Ganguro" look of the 1990s consisted of very tanned skin with lightened hair, and certain kinds of eye makeup. The "Kogals" conspicuously display fashion accessories and technological gadgets. Adopting these looks and these lifestyles helps distinguish individual Japanese people from the thousands of other people with whom they share cities and streets; cosplay is a refuge of color and distinction in a society of stark sameness.

Of course, one of the main characteristics of the cosplay subculture is that observers can easily identify to which group a participant belongs. The new identity is as carefully crafted to fit in with the understood rules as it is a rebellion against the norm. A fashion is, after all, a style of dress used by many other people; a teenager dressed in Goth Lolita clothing will be virtually indistinguishable from other Goth Lolitas to an outside observer. On the one hand, costumes enable wearers to set themselves apart from the crowd. On the other, choosing a group to follow is a behavior that the costume was supposed to undermine in the first place.

The following chapter explores the conflicts between such modern expressions of life and the traditional ways of the larger population in Japanese society, including positive and negative consequences.

| "*Entrepreneurship is the most satisfying path for a smart, ambitious woman [in Japan]."*

Entrepreneurs Are Succeeding in Japan

Veronica Chambers

Veronica Chambers spent several months in Japan on a fellowship from the Japan Society conducting research. She has been an editor for The New York Times Magazine, *a culture writer for* Newsweek, *and is the author of several books. The following viewpoint is an excerpt from* Kickboxing Geishas: How Modern Japanese Women Are Changing Their Nation, *a nonfiction portrayal of Japanese women who are breaking out of traditional, restrictive roles by challenging stereotypes and claiming new positions and power in Japanese society.*

As you read, consider the following questions:

1. What personal benefits does entrepreneurship offer to working women in Japan, according to Chambers?

2. What gaps in the Japanese consumer market do Yoko Shimizu's jewelry and Web site fill, in the author's view?

Veronica Chambers, "Outside of Corporate Japan", in *Kickboxing Geishas: How Modern Japanese Women Are Changing Their Nation.* New York, NY: Free Press (Simon & Schuster), 2007. Copyright © 2007 by Veronica Chambers. Reproduced by permission of Free Press, an imprint of Simon & Schuster.

3. According to Chambers, how has Tomoko Yachi's success as the proprietor of a coffee shop benefited the lives of other women in her community?

At thirty-two, Kay Otsuka is almost as old as the publication she now edits. She tells me that the magazine first debuted in 1970 as *The Job Guide for Women*. Women weren't really in the workplace at this time, and the magazine was more of a statistical abstract of how many women worked in different fields. In the 1980s, the magazine was reborn again as *The Catalogue of Female Jobs*. The covers featured illustrations of women dressed as photographers, businesswomen, golfers. It had a very "You've come a long way, baby" feel to it. The magazine became more prescriptive: featuring articles on how women could get a job, how to choose a career field, and what women need to do to get ahead. This second stage of the magazine featured a sixteen-page color insert on career women of the day and maybe two hundred pages of newsprint. Now in its *Slow Work, Slow Life* incarnation, which debuted in 2005, the magazine is all color, all aspirational profiles. "The magazine now features famous women," Kay explains. "Our readers want to know how they got there, and what their lives are like." She says the magazine is called *Slow Work, Slow Life* because the emphasis isn't on corporate Japan. "The focus is on jobs which provide the opportunity for slow life, which is life as they wish." . . .

Entrepreneurial Revolutionaries

As an editor at a magazine about women and work, Kay has been tracking the rumblings of this revolution for seven years. "In the early stages, it was just a small number of women who had careers at big companies. In the beginning, they got a lot of attention from the media," she explains. "Nowadays, women working for small and medium companies are quite active. The biggest growth is in women who have started their own businesses. They have chosen to have more time and a schedule they can arrange for themselves. Women are becoming more flexible and better at arranging their lives, so they can live as they wish."

The key for women around the world, of course, is how to balance the private and the professional life. Kay points out that there's somewhat of an answer in how we talk about our jobs. You may never meet a woman who says, "I've got a perfectly balanced life." But as in music, the true melody can be found in the silence between the notes. "The early career women pushed us to do what they did—work really really hard," Kay says. "Their motto was "*Gambate!*" or "Go for it!" Today, women are working hard, they are just not showing their sweat as a badge of honor."

While she says that more and more recent university graduates are finding a place in big companies, entrepreneurship is the most satisfying path for a smart, ambitious woman. "What editing this magazine has taught me is that women who have the power and energy to do it, choose to open their own businesses," she says. "These women are just not going to wait for corporate Japan to change. The crucial point is that women need to take care of themselves and they need to feel like they are most important. Traditionally, Japanese women don't really put their wishes ahead of a man's. You know the stereotype, not really outspoken, very obedient."

There's a term for the this kind of woman, *yamato-nodeshiko*, which means "nice, sensitive, polite woman who follows." Kay says, "That's the kind of women who was appreciated in Japan. I'm not sure when that tradition changed, or if it has really changed. But the women we feature in our magazine express what they want by speaking out. At first, women were afraid to speak out. If they wanted to do a job, they didn't know how to make their dreams come true. But they found that when they spoke out, they were guided onto the right track." . . .

Women in Business

Traditional Japanese low social expectations for women actually seem to encourage women to start their own businesses. They are able to tackle challenges without feeling pressure from the burdens that Japanese men typically bear with regard to social and financial obligations for their families. The stigma associated with a woman who chooses a career in the corporate business world over family does not exist for women entrepreneurs. Women have the freedom to start their own businesses without risking loss of income for their families.

Evidence suggests that Japanese women have more potential for becoming entrepreneurs than do men. For example, in 2004, the National Life Finance Corporation of Japan conducted an entrepreneurship survey titled "Wake Up Japan, Dream Gate Project" among all people who were considering starting their own business within one year. . . . The fear of losing or decreasing income was cited by 26.8 percent of the respondents as the primary concern preventing them from becoming entrepreneurs. The obligation of supporting a family overwhelmed 16.5 percent of the respondents. . . .

Since Japanese women have traditionally played the supporting roles in their families and society, rather than the primary role of securing income, Japanese women may be in a better position than men with regard to taking the risk of becoming entrepreneurs. Consequently, Japanese women increasingly see entrepreneurship as a viable option for themselves.

Charla Griffy-Brown and Noriko Oakland,
Graziadio Business Repost, *vol. 10, 2007.*

Turning Passion into a Profession

Jewelry designer Yoko Shimizu has plenty to say. She's in her early forties, with rock-star hair, bright blue turquoise stone rings, a black leather jacket with asymmetrical lapels, and four long silver necklaces hanging from her delicate neck. Her company, Balance +, sells Yoko's designs, both as completed jewelry you can buy as is and as jewelry kits, which you can assemble yourself. This "do-it-yourself" idea is new to Japan and Yoko has come along with the right idea at the right time. Thirty-five thousand individual users visit her Web site every day. Her office in the chic Aoyama neighborhood is bustling with more than a dozen employees. And because she understands that trends move quickly in Japan, she puts new designs and new kits on her Web site every week. The inspiration for her business, she tells me, was simple. "I love jewelry. I love stones," she says. "In Japan, there are many kinds of jewelry shops. But the kind of jewelry that is sold in shops is too childish for women in their thirties and forties to wear. I felt like I could step into the gap."

She had the background to do it, having designed jewelry for a popular Japanese brand called 4° as well as for Sotheby's. She had also been a graphic designer as well as produced events for the Guggenheim Museum. "All along, jewelry has been my focus," she says. "I needed to work as an employee. But I was unsatisfied because I have my own ideas and my own creativity. I let people know about my ideas and I started to make jewelry. I have a lot of friends who are editors and stylists; they got my stuff out there. Then I just went with the flow." Four years ago [2003], she launched her own company. Soon after she published her first book called *Beads and Accessories*. . . .

Women Solving Problems for Women

Two hours outside of Tokyo, in a residential town called Saitama, there's a café called Choco Bagel shop. The owner is a young woman called Tomoko Yachi, and the café is located on the first floor of her house. Tomoko has auburn hair and she's dressed in the casual-but-funky style of a woman who does a lot of running around but really, really loves clothes. She is wearing a white lace shirt underneath a black cardigan. She's also wearing khaki pants with a long black skirt thrown over them. Her café, which she and her husband built all by themselves, including all the construction and painting, is an homage to shabby chic. It's more like the kind of place you'd find in a beachside community in the Hamptons than in a town so spread out that the taxi driver cannot find it amidst all the fields. Everything is decorated in shades of white from yellowish cream to the palest caramel: clapboard walls, muslin curtains, painted wooden floors, chairs, and tables. The café actually grew out of a small fancy-foods gift shop (the only place in Saitama, for example, where you can buy caviar and Sarabeth's jam) that Tomoko runs in the converted barn next to the house.

"After running the store next door for a year, I realized that many customers with kids wanted a comfortable place to sit and have a cup of tea," Tomoko says. "I myself was hesitant to go to cafés with my own daughter, so I wanted to provide a safe space for my customers and that's what this is." Tomoko's store has been open for four years, and the café has been open for three. . . .

As Tomoko pours me a cup of *yuzu* tea, Japanese citrus rinds steamed with honey, and pours herself a cup of coffee, I realize that she is living the *Slow Work, Slow Life* ideal that I have been longing for since I first came to Japan. She laughs when I tell her that I've completely changed my own life plan. I want to move to Saitama and open up a café. She goes into another room and returns with a stack of books that were her inspiration in opening up the shop and later, the café. The titles range from *The Relaxed Home* to *Family Living* to *At Peace at Home*. Tomoko says, "I thought a lot about the kind of environment I wanted to create for my work life. I have so many responsibilities. I'm married, I have a career, I have a child. I think it's very important for me to have fun while I'm doing my work. Taking care of my daughter, especially, is a lot of hard work and responsibility."

The café is open only three days a week, from 11 A.M. to 4 P.M. Tomoko planned the hours around her daughter's school schedule. As if on cue, seven-year-old Natsumi—whose name means "summer ocean" Tomoko tells me—comes bouncing in. One of the two employees at work in the café makes Natsumi a cup of hot chocolate and she happily starts on her homework. Tomoko still remembers the days when the café sat empty for days at a time. Now, she says, it's very successful. "I feel so sad because in the beginning, I could remember all the customers names and faces," Tomoko says. "Now I just smile because I have no idea who all of these women are."

A Legacy of Working Women

Tomoko grew up in Saitama. Her parents owned a soba [Japanese noodle] restaurant, not far from her own café. "When I was my daughter's age," she remembers fondly. "I was always talking to the customers and bringing them tea. I really liked the soba place. When I was a girl, on Saturdays, school finished at noon. The only thing I hated was that they served soba every Saturday at school. I was sick of soba!" Her whole family worked at the restaurant and her grandmother made tempura. "As a woman, I grew up knowing that my mother and grandmother were working, so for me it was very natural that I would one day work too," she says. "My husband does not have very conventional ideas about women staying home to do housework. He understands that I have to work outside of the home."

Tomoko's Choco Bagel Shop and Café has not only made her an entrepreneur, but created opportunities for other women in the community as well. The café has two employees and the shop employs one other full-time employee. "All of the employees are working mothers," Tomoko says. "If they have special events, sporting events, a meeting at the school, we discuss it among the workers and we adjust the schedule. I can understand their situation because I'm a mother, too. As a working mother, I'm really concerned about all of my employees' kids. If it were a regular company, it would be very hard to say, 'I've got to go home. I'm concerned because my kid is sick.'" Tomoko's daughter comes in and takes a seat on her lap. At the same time that Tomoko is understanding of her employees' situation as working mothers, she has no problem dealing with other management issues that may arise, be it tardiness or poor performance. "I'm very frank," Tomoko says. "I say what I need to say as a boss. I consider the staff to be not just employees, but my business partners. If something is hurting the business, I'm going to bring it up."

She says that having the café open three days a week, "is the perfect schedule for me. Because the café is open three days a week, I can concentrate on my work and give it my full focus." On Mondays, she prepares for the week. She spends a great deal of the day baking cakes and making lunches. The café is open Tuesdays, Wednesdays, and Thursdays. Fridays, she says, "are just for me. Sometimes I visit other cafés, sometimes I just stay at home and relax. Saturdays and Sundays are for my family." She admits that she doesn't manage to have every Friday to herself, but she makes it a priority, "at least twice a month." I know it's hard work, but it also sounds idyllic. The "Slow Life" movement comes to life.

| "Japan scores poorly on almost every measure of entrepreneurship."

Business Traditions Cause Most Japanese Entrepreneurs to Fail

The Economist

The Economist *is an international weekly newspaper that presents a variety of positions on topics ranging from politics to culture from liberal and conservative perspectives. The following viewpoint first appeared as a special report on business in Japan. It contrasts the entrepreneurial environments of the United States and Japan, pointing out that the latter's business atmosphere does not encourage entrepreneurism.*

As you read, consider the following questions:

1. How do the characteristics of the Japanese labor market affect the likelihood of someone starting a new company, according to the author?

2. What steps does the *Economist* say the Japanese government has taken to encourage research and innovation in certain industries?

3. What effect would a stronger Japanese economy have on the progress of its entrepreneurial culture, in the author's opinion?

Takashi Masuda wiggles his finger next to an apparently random collage of tinsel, cuddly toys and cutlery, illuminated by a spotlight. A small black chip, glued to a plastic ruler, is propped up nearby, with wires running to a circuit board festooned with blinking red lights. From this another cable runs to a large high-definition TV where every ridge of the skin on Mr Masuda's finger, every twinkly highlight on the tinsel and every hair on the cuddly toys can be clearly seen.

Mr Masuda's company, Acutelogic, makes specialist image-processing chips and software for digital cameras. Its newest product, which picked up every nuance of Mr Masuda's wiggling finger, is a tiny high-definition video sensor that can fit into a mobile phone. The idea is to make camcorders obsolete, says Mr Masuda.

He founded Acutelogic after leaving Sony, where he worked on the team that created the Cyber-shot digital camera. He felt that the electronics giant's management had lost its way and wanted to start his own company. So he set up Acutelogic, with venture-capital funding, some investment from Fujitsu, a computer giant, and money raised from friends and family.

All this sounds very similar to the way things are done in America's Silicon Valley, where large firms such as IBM, Oracle, Sun and Hewlett-Packard often act as unofficial "incubators" for engineers who spend a few years learning the ropes and then leave to set up on their own. But Mr Masuda's story differs in one crucial respect: he was 50 when he left Sony, and was able to make the leap because he was offered an early-retirement package. "It would have been better to do it at 40," he says. But had he done so, he would have lost his company pension. His story illustrates not how easy it is to start a company in Japan, but how difficult.

Japan scores poorly on almost every measure of entrepreneurship. It has the second-lowest level in the OECD [Organisation for Economic Co-operation and Development] of venture-capital investment as a share of GDP [gross domestic product], and what little venture capital is available goes disproportionately into existing firms rather than start-ups. Venture-capital investment in Japan amounts to some $2 billion a year, around a tenth of the figure in America. Start-ups account for 4% of all firms, compared with 10% in Europe and 14% in America. Japan also came last in the International Institute for Management Development's rankings on entrepreneurship and second-last in the Global Entrepreneurship Monitor's ranking of early-stage entrepreneurial activity (defined as the proportion of people of working age who are involved in such activity). Why?

Cultural factors are a big part of the explanation. As a hoary old Japanese saying has it, "the nail that sticks out is hammered down." Conformity is valued over individualism. "Students work hard at school, but they learn how to take tests, not how to think," laments Sakie Fukushima of Korn/Ferry. And unlike American culture, which venerates the maverick self-made millionaire and is tolerant of failure, Japan frowns upon public displays of wealth and stigmatises business failure.

On the Outer Edge

Take Takafumi Horie, an example of the sort of entrepreneur who remains extremely rare in Japan. With his characteristic jeans, sneakers and spiky hair, this self-styled rebel against Japan's corporate establishment transformed his internet start-up, aptly named Livin' On The Edge, into a vast conglomerate, which he renamed livedoor in 2004. At its peak, livedoor was worth some ¥930 billion [yen] ([US] $8 billion) and owned an accounting-software firm, an internet travel agency, a securities house and a second-hand car business.

In 2005 Mr Horie mounted a takeover bid for Nippon Broadcasting System, a radio station, which would have given him control of Fuji Television, Japan's biggest commercial television station. The battle ended in a truce between Fuji and livedoor, but Mr Horie had infuriated the business establishment. In January 2006 raids on his home and office were broadcast live on television, and in March [2007] he was convicted of fraud and sentenced to two-and-a-half years in jail.

Mr Horie's critics regarded his use of elaborate financial engineering as evidence that pro-market reforms had gone too far; his supporters claimed that the attack on his empire had been orchestrated by Japan's corporate old guard. But his fate sent a clear signal to anyone who regarded Mr Horie as a new role model for Japanese entrepreneurs, says Hirotaka Takeuchi, dean of the school of corporate strategy at Hitotsubashi University. "He showed you can be an entrepreneur and be successful, but you shouldn't take it to excess. You've got to abide by the rules."

In truth, Mr Horie was not the American-style capitalist people imagined him to be; indeed, the way he concealed the precarious financial state of his sprawling empire reeked of old-style Japanese book-cooking. But his behaviour served to reinforce the traditional Japanese scepticism towards showy entrepreneurs.

Restricted by Corporate Culture

"If you stand out too much you become a target," says Yoshito Hori, a venture capitalist [VC] and the founder of Globis Management School, a business school. That alone persuades many entrepreneurs to keep a low profile. But they face more than just cultural obstacles: the rigidity of the Japanese labour market makes life that much harder for them. Anyone who leaves a regular job for a start-up will find it difficult to get another job if the venture fails. And pensions are a particular problem: as Mr Masuda's example shows, people working for large companies are reluctant to leave their jobs in their 30s and 40s because they will lose their retirement benefits.

Other difficulties facing entrepreneurs include the lack of venture-capital funding, a dearth of knowledgeable angel investors, difficulty in hiring experienced managers and a lack of support networks, says Joichi Ito, an internet investor with experience both in Japan and in Silicon Valley. This forces some entrepreneurs to rely on foreign funding. "VCs and entrepreneurs are not as professional as they are in Silicon Valley," says Sachio Semmoto, the entrepreneur behind a series of successful Japanese telecoms firms. Goldman Sachs, an American investment bank, put $25m [million] into his most recent venture, whereas local Japanese venture funds contributed just a few hundred thousand dollars.

Given the innovative prowess of Japan's industrial giants, does it matter if start-ups have a hard time? The Economist Intelligence Unit ranked Japan first in a recent study of innovation, based on the number of patents awarded per million people. Japan generates 51% more patents than America in absolute terms, which works out at around 3.5 times as many patents per person. It also has more scientific researchers per million people (5,900 compared with 4,200 for America) and a higher research-and-development (R&D) intensity, at 3.4% of GDP compared with 2.8% for America.

But things may not be as rosy as these numbers suggest. Patents are an imperfect proxy for innovation; Japan's armies of researchers spend more time than their foreign counterparts on non-research activities such as administration, which reduces their effectiveness; and a report by the Cabinet Office found that the effectiveness of Japan's private-sector R&D— the ratio of operating profits to R&D expenditure—declined throughout the 1990s.

Entrepreneurial Rates in Various Countries, 2007

Nation	Nascent Entrepreneurial Activity (%)	New Business Owner-Managers (%)	Early State Entrepreneurial Activity (%)	Established Business Owner-Managers (%)	Overall Entrepreneurial Activity (%)
Hong Kong	5.7	4.3	10.0	5.6	15.0
Israel	3.6	2.0	5.4	2.4	7.4
Sweden	1.9	2.4	4.2	4.7	8.8
United Kingdom	2.9	2.7	5.5	5.1	10.5
United Arab Emirates	4.6	4.1	8.4	3.4	11.8
Japan	**2.2**	**2.2**	**4.3**	**8.7**	**12.6**
India	6.0	2.6	8.5	5.5	13.9
United States	6.5	3.4	9.6	5.0	14.1
China	6.9	10.0	16.4	8.4	24.6
Thailand	9.4	18.6	26.9	21.4	47.4

TAKEN FROM: Neils Bosma et al., "Table 1: Prevalence Rates of Entrepreneurial Activity and Business Owner-Managers across Countries 2007, Ages 18–64," *Global Entrepreneurship Monitor 2007 Executive Report.*

Wrong Side of Trends

All this has fuelled concerns that Japan might now be on the wrong side of several trends. Japan's most famous innovations, such as the Sony Walkman and the Toyota Prius, originated in big companies. But the internet boom highlighted the vibrancy of the American way of innovating, in which a host of entrepreneurial start-ups try out risky new ideas and the most successful of them either become, or are acquired by, larger firms. The American approach supports radical technological breakthroughs but depends on plenty of risk capital.

Akira Takeishi of the Institute of Innovation Research at Hitotsubashi University has investigated why Japanese firms are highly competitive in some industries (carmaking, electronics, imaging products, video games) and less so in others (personal computers, software). He concluded that Japanese firms did best in manufacturing industries with closed product designs that do not require collaboration with the rest of the industry, and worst in fields based on open standards and modular architectures. So if the nature of innovation has changed, and it now depends on collaboration with other firms around the world, Japan could be in trouble. Japanese patents with foreign co-inventors accounted for less than 3% of the total, compared with 12% in America.

Another worry is that Japanese companies concentrate too much on incremental innovations rather than radical breakthroughs. This served them well in the second half of the 20th century. But given the disruptive impact of the internet and the need for entirely new energy technologies to mitigate climate change, it may no longer be the right thing to do.

The government has formulated a series of plans and targets, including measures to boost international co-operation and increased funding for researchers in fields such as nanotechnology and clean energy, where breakthroughs could open up big new markets. It has also set about improving the climate for entrepreneurs and start-ups, for example by offering more favourable tax treatment for venture-capital investments, reducing the minimum capital requirement for new businesses to ¥1 and making it easier for start-ups to issue share options to staff.

Land of Opportunity?

One sign of progress is the higher turnover of new firms. Between 1997 and 2004 an average of 99 new companies a year were listed in Japan, up from 26 a year in 1981–89 and 36 a year in 1990–96. The number of delistings also rose, from four or five a year in the 1980s and early 1990s to an average of 41 a year in 1997–2004. This is due in part to the rise of second-tier stockmarkets such as Mothers in Tokyo and Hercules in Osaka, and the loosening of listing requirements on JASDAQ [Japan Association of Securities Dealers Automated Quotation], which has made it easier for start-ups to go public. Mr Hori notes that there were 747 IPOs [initial public offerings] in Japan between 2001 and 2005, compared with 617 in America.

The slightly more flexible labour market has made it easier for start-ups to attract skilled workers. "Things are changing—people are coming out of big firms to join us," says Mr Masuda, whose firm has hired engineers from JVC, Canon and other electronics giants. He says start-ups also offer more opportunities and better prospects to Chinese and South Korean engineering students in Japan: "We evaluate people for their skills, not their skins and eyes."

Mr Hori goes so far as to suggest that start-ups have played an unacknowledged role in helping to turn around Japan's economy in recent years. He says the rebound was partly driven by the emergence of new companies in knowledge-based industries, led by entrepreneurs in their 20s and 30s. He points to Rakuten, an internet-shopping firm that now has a market capitalisation of nearly $6 billion, making it one of the largest internet-commerce firms in the world. Other Japanese success stories include DeNA, an internet-auction and shopping site, and Mixi, a social-networking site. Mr Ito is heartened by Japan's latest crop of internet entrepreneurs, such as Mixi's Kenji Kasahara. "The new generation of internet CEOs [chief executive officers] are very humble. They don't spend all their money in [the] Ginza [commercial district] buying cars," he says.

It seems that entrepreneurs can do well in Japan as long as they do not draw too much attention to themselves. Mr Hori thinks they have excellent prospects. There are still relatively few of them, and productivity in Japan's service sector is notoriously low, offering plenty of opportunities for start-ups. He says 70% of his venture-capital investments are in services companies, from nursing homes to wedding planning. Apart from services, says Mr Hori, "we are betting on areas where Japan has an edge," such as mobile technology, optics, robotics, digital animation and video games.

Some Worries Remain

Despite these hopeful signs, however, some worries remain. One concern is that if economic growth strengthens and more full-time jobs are created, would-be entrepreneurs may be tempted to take the safer option of a job instead. Japan's recent wave of entrepreneurship, suggests Randall Jones at the OECD, was caused in part by the lack of job opportunities for talented graduates during the hiring freeze of the 1990s. But Mr Hori insists that times have changed, and "the best and brightest are now going into the entrepreneurial field, which has never happened before."

Another concern is that too much government effort to encourage start-ups and promote innovation is concentrated on manufacturing and technology rather than services, which is arguably where change is most needed. To keep the momentum going, the OECD recommends reductions in capital-gains tax to encourage venture capital; more portable pensions and performance-based pay for researchers to encourage mobility between academia and industry; a broader educational curriculum; and the promotion of cross-border trade and investment, since good ideas often come from abroad. Changing Japanese attitudes to entrepreneurship will take time and further reforms, but at least the wheels have started turning.

> *"The traditional diet in Japan is built around ... rice and other grains, ... vegetables and fruits, and also fish, but relatively little animal fat, meat and sweets."*

The Traditional Lifestyle Has Kept Obesity Low in Japan

Benjamin Senauer and Masahiko Gemma

Benjamin Senauer is a professor of applied economics and the former codirector of The Food Industry Center at the University of Minnesota's St. Paul campus. Masahiko Gemma is a professor at the School of Social Sciences at Waseda University in Tokyo. In the following viewpoint the authors highlight the significant differences between health factors in Japan and the United States, finding that the Japanese diet includes healthier foods and fewer calories than the typical American diet and that the Japanese walk more than Americans do.

As you read, consider the following questions:

1. In 2002, according to the authors, how did the average Japanese caloric intake compare with that of Americans in 2001–2002?

Benjamin Senauer and Masahiko Gemma, "Reducing Obesity: What Americans Can Learn from the Japanese," *Choices Magazine*, vol. 21, no. 4, 2006, pp. 265–268. Copyright © 1999–2008 Choices Magazine and the Agricultural & Applied Economics Association.

2. What are some characteristics of the typical Japanese meal, as cited by Senauer and Gemma?

3. Why does the average Japanese person walk so many steps each day, according to the authors?

Japan has one of the lower rates of obesity, although it is increasing virtually everywhere, and the United States has one of the highest rates of obesity in the world. Only 3.6% of Japanese age 15 and over had a Body Mass Index (BMI) over 30 in 2002, which is the international standard and is determined by dividing a person's weight in kilograms by their height in meters squared. In contrast, 32.0% of Americans age 20 and over were obese, and a total of 66% were either overweight (BMI over 25) or obese in 2003–04; some two-thirds of the adult population. Because the distribution of body fat affects health risks and Asians tend to have more abdominal fat at lower BMI levels, the Japanese government uses a BMI over 25 to define obesity. For Japanese age 20 and over, the same age group as for the U.S., 25.6% had a BMI over 25, which is still lower than the U.S. rate. Much can be learned about how to reduce obesity in the United States if we can explain why the rate is so much lower in Japan.

Being obese and overweight is associated with an increased risk of many chronic diseases and premature death, plus significant increases in health care costs. Viewed at its simplest, a person gains weight when their caloric intake exceeds the calories expended through basic metabolism and physical activity. The average person in Japan both eats less and is more physically active than the typical American.

Caloric Intakes and Availability

The average daily intake of Japanese over one year old was 1,930 calories in 2002, whereas Americans ages 1–85 consumed 2,168 calories on average in 2001–02. The typical adult in Japan is smaller in stature than the average American, thus obviously needing fewer calories. However, this factor explains only a modest portion of the difference of over 200 daily calories. Moreover, the average daily fat consumption in Japan was 54.4 grams, compared to 80.6 grams in the United States.

Food balance sheets, also referred to as food supply and utilization data, can be used to compare the per capita availability of calories back to 1960 in the two countries. The quantities of food available at retail are derived by applying conversion factors, which account for losses in processing and distribution, to the estimated supply of each agricultural commodity, such as potatoes. The nutrients across all food categories are aggregated to determine the nutrients available for consumption. The calories available rose only slightly in Japan between 1960 and 2003, from 2,291 to 2,558. Over the same period, the U.S. per capita availability of calories increased from 3,100 in 1960 to a rather astounding 3,900 in 2003. While the increase from 1960 to 2003 was only 267 calories per capita in Japan, in the United States it was 800 calories per person. As expected, these figures are higher than actual caloric intake, which was provided in the previous paragraph. However, this data does suggest the sheer abundance of food, especially calorie dense food, Americans have available and, hence, are tempted by. A reflection of this is the "supersizing" of serving portions, with many Americans losing any sense of what a normal serving size should be. . . .

Strong Dietary Traditions

The traditional diet in Japan is built around a base of rice and other grains, with plentiful consumption of vegetables and fruits, and also fish, but relatively little animal fat, meat and sweets. In Japan, the presentation of the food is very important, and particular attention is given to the colors and textures. There is an old Japanese saying, "we eat with our eyes." Portions are much smaller at Japanese restaurants or in home-prepared meals than is typical in the United States. An elegant

Obesity Rates by Country, 2005

Nations with the Highest Obesity Rates

Rank	Country	Rate of Obesity
1	United States	30.6%
2	Mexico	24.2%
3	United Kingdom	23%
4	Slovakia	22.4%
5	Greece	21.9%

Nations with the Lowest Obesity Rates

Rank	Country	Rate of Obesity
1	**Japan**	**3.2%**
1	South Korea	3.2%
2	Switzerland	7.7%
3	Norway	8.3%
4	Italy	8.5%
5	Austria	9.1%

TAKEN FROM: "Table 5: Obesity, percentage of adult population with a BMI>30kg//m2," Organisation for Economic Co-Operation and Development: Directorate for Employment, Labour, and Social Affairs, June 5, 2005.

dining experience might consist of dozens of small dishes, some no more than a few bites. The meal is meant to be beautiful, as well as delicious. Fruit is usually served at the end, rather than a rich dessert. Traditionally in eating, the Japanese have applied the concept of *enryo* (restraint). Although more Western foods are being eaten, traditional food customs are still quite strong in Japan.

On a recent visit to a daycare facility in Tokyo by the authors, the careful attention to the nutritional quality of the food provided was impressive. A sample lunch is placed under a glass cover for all the parents to see as they pick their children up at the end of the day. A newsletter provides the meal plan to the parents in advance and suggests foods to serve at home to nutritionally complement those provided at the daycare. In addition, unlike in most American schools, students are taught even at an early age to appreciate and respect food. The students must wash their hands before eating and are expected to use good table manners. They sit at low tables with small chairs and are served their trays individually. Before eating, they thank the farmers who grew the food and those who prepared it. . . .

A Different Culture of Activity

Japanese walk much more in their daily lives than Americans. Walking is a simple, but effective form of exercise in which everyone except the disabled can engage. The average person in Japan, 15 years old and above, walked 7,421 steps per day in 2002, about 3 3/4 miles at 2,000 steps per mile. Men walked an average of 7,573 steps and women 7,140. A recent nationally representative survey of Americans on walking by Harris Survey found that men walked an average of 5,940 steps and women 5,276. Pedometers were provided to participants in both surveys that counted their steps. The average length of a step for the Japanese may be less than for the average American, who is taller, but only modestly so.

The Japanese walk an average of about 2,000 steps more per day than Americans, which burns about 100 additional calories. The reason they walk more is they rely far less on automobiles and far more on mass transit to get around. The use of public transportation usually entails walking, since it does not take you from the door of your home to that of your workplace or other destination. Americans who commute to work in their cars or drive to go shopping may simply drive from their garage and then park only a few hundred feet or less from their workplace or the shopping mall, doing whatever they can to minimize any walking. Moreover, in crowded Japanese cities, the easiest way to get somewhere nearby is to simply walk. . . .

A Simple Solution

The key lessons from Japan are that Americans need to eat less, giving more attention to the quality of food and less to the quantity, and get more exercise, particularly by adding more walking to their daily lives.

| "[A] fat farm is part of a broad range of programs instituted by companies and the government . . . as Japan begins its battle with the bulge."

Modern Dietary Changes Have Created Obesity-Related Health Problems in Japan

Rena Singer

Rena Singer is a journalist based in Jerusalem. She has written for the Philadelphia Inquirer *as well as* The Boston Globe, USA Today, *and* U.S. News & World Report. *In the following viewpoint, Singer describes the controversial reaction by the Japanese government to the rise in obesity and its attendant diseases, such as diabetes and heart disease, among the people of Japan. The author also discusses the government's solutions to this social problem.*

As you read, consider the following questions:

1. What changes in health and food consumption have triggered the Japanese government's interest in its population's health, according to Singer?

Rena Singer, "Japan Cracks Down on Waistlines," *U.S. News & World Report*, vol. 144, June 4, 2008, pp. 1–3. Copyright © 2008 U.S. News and World Report, L.P. All rights reserved. Reprinted with permission.

2. With what measurement does the author say the government will officially evaluate the health of individual citizens?

3. According to Singer why are some Japanese people angry about these new government regulations?

Sunstar Inc., makers of GUM and Butler brand oral hygiene products, will be sending select employees to a most unusual three-day company retreat [in 2008]. The goal isn't high productivity, product development, or team building but instead slim waistlines. Sunstar's fat farm is part of a broad range of programs instituted by companies and the government here as Japan begins its battle with the bulge.

In a country seemingly devoid of Rubenesque curves, a country in which tofu makes regular appearances on menus and bean paste serves as a common substitute for chocolates in desserts, a country with the best longevity rates in the world, this may seem a strange preoccupation. But the two-hour lines at Tokyo's Krispy Kreme doughnut shops and the rising rates of diabetes tell of a country in transition.

Indeed, rice and fresh fruit consumption in Japan has fallen by about half since 1970, while beef consumption is up more than 40 percent and coffee drinking has tripled. The crepe shops that have sprouted up on street corners throughout Tokyo demonstrate the growing appetite for sweets. Notably, the number of diabetics in Japan has doubled in the past 15 years, and the government estimates that a further 10 million people have the warning signs for the disease. This is particularly troubling in a rapidly aging country like Japan, adding to the strain on Japan's national health insurance program.

Government Health Standards

Japan's Ministry of Health, Labor, and Welfare released an alarming study [in 2006] that found that half of all men between the ages of 40 and 74 and 1 in 5 women in the same age group showed signs of "metabolic syndrome"—a cluster of risk factors for heart attacks and cardiovascular disease that includes high cholesterol, high blood pressure, elevated insulin levels, and abdominal obesity.

The report shocked the nation and prompted the government to pass legislation to force the Japanese to shape up. The laws to address what the Japanese have come to call "metabo" [took] effect [in 2008]. They've given the government and employers, long dominant forces in Japanese workers' lives, places at the dinner table in ordinary Japanese homes. They've also sparked a flurry of products to help Japanese keep trim or shed extra pounds.

One regulation requires all citizens over the age of 40 to have their waists measured every year. If a man's waist is more than 33.5 inches or a woman's more than 35.5 inches, they are considered at risk and referred for counseling and close monitoring. The government is also requiring companies to slim down their workers or face higher payments into the national insurance program.

Employers Get Involved

Companies across the country have responded with a variety of initiatives. Sunstar has its boot camp, which includes lectures on diet, exercise, and even Zen meditation. Family members of employees over 40 whose love handles won't budge will also be asked to attend the camp. The company also offers overweight workers free delivery of healthful, traditionally Japanese food like soybeans and brown rice.

Computer, mobile phone, and appliance maker NEC requires all of its employees in its Japanese offices to undergo yearly checks from the time they turn 30, a full decade earlier than the government regulations require. And all employees must attend lifestyle instruction courses. Any employee who shows "poor results" (think beer belly) will receive individual

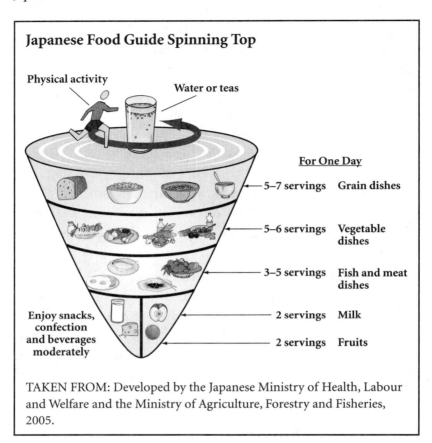

Japanese Food Guide Spinning Top

Physical activity

Water or teas

For One Day

5–7 servings Grain dishes

5–6 servings Vegetable dishes

3–5 servings Fish and meat dishes

Enjoy snacks, confection and beverages moderately

2 servings Milk

2 servings Fruits

TAKEN FROM: Developed by the Japanese Ministry of Health, Labour and Welfare and the Ministry of Agriculture, Forestry and Fisheries, 2005.

follow-up attention, says Susumu Makihara, general manager of human resources for the global giant's Japan operations.

NEC's cafeteria now sports a "healthy menu option," and Makihara says that for now, the company will not be monitoring what employees eat in the cafeteria. "This is a major issue for aging societies," says Makihara. "NEC is facing this now and going beyond what is required by the law, though we recognize that, at the end of the day, it is a personal choice."

Other companies have made healthful eating less of a recommendation and more of a job requirement. The local press highlighted one corporation, a seafood processor, that will require its staff to eat at least one of the company's own fish sausages every day. The sausages contain an omega-3 fatty acid called DHA, which is believed to reduce the risk of cardiovascular disease.

Individuals React

Few Japanese are willing to criticize the government's regulations or their employer's plans for the record. But the *Japan Times* newspaper ran a column quoting outraged, but unnamed, workers. One worker says he intends to fast for three days before his examination to shed the inches he needs to pass his physical. Another told the newspaper, "My waistline is none of my company's business."

Many Japanese have turned to technology to fight flab. Television here is now flush with commercials for exercise equipment and electronic belts that promise to melt the fat away. And NEC has just developed a new feature for mobile phones in Japan, which analyzes the reported daily intake of the phone user and determines if the diet is healthful.

It is now a civic duty to stay fit, says Naoko Takase, assistant manager of public relations for Sunstar. "Many employees are happy for this information and guidance we offer in our program," he says. "But some employees think they want to do this themselves, that their diet is not the company or government's concern."

> "[Although one woman's husband had]
> asked for a simple ceremony . . . social
> pressure compelled her to go ahead with
> a standard Japanese funeral."

Japanese Funerals Are a Standardized Social Ritual

Andrew Bernstein

Andrew Bernstein is an associate professor of history at Lewis and Clark College in Portland, Oregon. In the following viewpoint, excerpted from his book Modern Passings: Death Rites, Politics, and Social Change in Imperial Japan, *Bernstein describes the evolution of Japan's funeral industry into the profit-driven market that it is today. Decisions are still largely in the hands of the living descendants, under the heavy influence and pressure of the often-manipulative undertakers and religious institutions, he points out.*

As you read, consider the following questions:

1. According to Bernstein, why were professional funeral managers first brought by individual families into the death and burial process?

Excerpted from "Epilogue: The Japanese Way of Death and Its Critics" by Andrew Bernstein, in *Modern Passings: Death Rites, Politics, and Social Change in Imperial Japan* (Honolulu, HI: University of Hawaii Press, 2006). Copyright © 2006 University of Hawaii Press. All rights reserved. Reproduced by permission.

2. Why are people like Mori Kenji calling for more government regulation of the Japanese burial system, according to the author?

3. What is one example that Bernstein gives of how unrelated people are using the inevitability of death to form social networks with each other in life?

Death in Japan today is handled through a format that is national in scope. There are local variations, to be sure, but these fit within a framework of death management that is recognizable throughout the country, whether in small-town Kyushu or downtown Tokyo. The individual elements of this framework evolved at different times and for different reasons. Centuries ago Buddhist priests developed religious practices, including reading sutras and offering incense, that still feature prominently in most Japanese funerals. Measures to guard against death pollution have also long been shared by communities across the archipelago.

It was not until Japan's transformation into a nation-state, however, that a standard scheme for handling the deceased fell into place. Although it initially threw it's support behind the Shinto funeral movement, within less than a decade the Meiji government abandoned its ill-fated effort to manipulate private ritual, choosing instead to acknowledge (to a self-serving extent) a separation between religion and the state. In the process it bureaucratized the management of physical remains. Detached from religious ritual, this management fell under the regulatory control of the Home Ministry, which ordered all deaths to be certified by doctors and reported to local officials. The ministry also established national guidelines for cremation, burial, and the use of graveyards. Government policies were adjusted to local realities, but combined with the forces of urbanization and the desires of a growing middle class, they engendered a standard method of cremation and burial that has made the sight of "soul parks" filled with family graves and their cremated remains a familiar one across Japan.

After it pulled out of the Shinto funeral movement, the state had little impact on the conduct of funerary rites that preceded and surrounded disposal of the dead, despite its support for thrift campaigns. Rather, it was the ascendant middle class, together with undertakers, who determined the format and conduct of modern funerals. Initially customers turned to undertakers to supply and coordinate lavish funeral processions, but as these became impractical due to street traffic, the funeral professionals created fixed (and private) ritual environments to replace them. During the 1920s and 1930s they also solidified their position by taking on responsibilities once delegated to family members and neighbors. It was, in fact, the ability of undertakers to help families cope with the dissolution of old social networks and plot the creation of new ones that fueled the development of a funeral industry that now markets a culture of ritual consumption nationwide. Because mourners do not want to risk slighting their guests and because guests feel most comfortable playing by clearly defined rules, bookstores are today filled with etiquette manuals training the ritually out-of-shape how to prepare for the marathon that is a Japanese funeral. Ultimately, however, it is only with the assistance of professionals that contemporary Japanese can bridge the gap between cultural expectations and the ritual knowledge needed to fulfill them. . . .

Power over the Bereaved

In the eyes of critics, . . . producers of funerals wield far more power than consumers and do not hesitate to take advantage of them. Since the late 1980s a steady stream of newspaper articles, televised news segments, and books has exposed the seamy business practices of Japanese undertakers, casting them in a light far harsher than the amusing glow of Itami [Jūzō's

Elaborate, Expensive, and Complicated

When it comes to honoring the dead, young, not-so-young and even very old Japanese appear united in their bafflement at the Buddhist funerals that are the most common means here of bidding a final, terminal farewell.

Many complain that rather than make the funeral a simple and heartfelt appeal to the gods to welcome the newly dead, families too often take it as an opportunity to show off, paying fortunes for lavish altars where coffins are dwarfed by floral displays, or for gravestones that are monumentally ostentatious. . . .

Eighty-one-year-old Teru Tanaka, whose husband died 25 years ago, has little patience with all the profligacy. "With our economy in such a rut, it's wasteful spending money on this stuff," she says. "The person's not even around any more."

Tanaka also complains about being obliged to attend funerals of distant acquaintances merely out of social obligation. With annual *koden* (obituary gifts) shelled out at funerals averaging almost 50,000 yen in Tokyo, it's easy to sympathize with Tanaka. And never mind that the average grave in Japan costs about 2.5 million yen, including the land-use fee and price of a stone marker.

Eric Prideaux, Japan Times, *October 27, 2002.*

1987 satire film *The Funeral*]. To give just one example, an undertaker turned critic published *Shitai wa shōhin!! warui sōgiya* (The corpse is a commodity!! Wicked undertakers) in 1992. Displaying the same indignation vented by customs reformers a century earlier, he mercilessly revealed dirty secrets of the trade. Among them is the system of paying off nurses and doctors at hospitals to gain access to the freshly dead and bereaved. Another is the practice of charging mourners according to fixed prices that disguise the true breakdown of costs involved in a funeral. The book emphasizes the insensitivity of money-hungry undertakers with sub-headings that include "The Target Commodity is the Corpse of a Small to Mid-sized Company President" and "A Child's Funeral Is Rather Savory."

Other books, such as *Anata no sōshiki, anata no ohaka* (Your funeral, your grave), encourage readers to create personalized ceremonies that do not reject undertakers, but instead make use of them. Breaking with convention might include, for instance, hiring a chamber group to play classical music instead of Buddhist priests to chant sutras. The movement to "do it your own way"—a phenomenon witnessed throughout the (post-) industrialized world—poses a challenge to the funeral industry, but like the shift from funeral processions to farewell ceremonies nearly a century earlier, it is one that forward looking undertakers can turn to their advantage. After all, they can just as well provide classical musicians as they can Buddhist priests, and in fact many have begun marketing individualized "nonreligious" (*mūshūkyō*) funerals in their company literature.

The popular reassessment of death rites in recent years extends to the grave, once again the focus of debates that call into question the boundaries negotiated between individuals, families, religious communities, and the state. Prominent among those challenging the current burial system is legal scholar Mori Kenji, author of *Haka to sōsō no genzai: Sōsen saishi kara sōsō no jiyū e* (Graves and funerals today: From ancestor worship to funereal freedom), who criticizes the postwar government for shirking what he sees as its duty to guarantee each citizen a secure resting place. The current civil code, like its Meiji predecessor, still places responsibility for the upkeep of tombs in the hands of individual families, ensuring that graves continue to go abandoned in large numbers. Inspired in part by Hosono Ungai's *Fumetsu no funbo*, Mori argues that the state should abandon this vestige of patrilineal control and instead establish stringent new rules for the maintenance of graves that are oriented toward protecting the rights of the deceased, not descendants.

Privatization of Religion

This call for increased regulation runs counter to the interests of Buddhist temples, who generally want to keep state interference to a minimum. The dismantling of state Shinto after World War II strengthened the hand of religious organizations seeking to assert their independence from government control. In this new environment Buddhist temples not only regained control of graveyards that had been seized during the Meiji period, they also won the right to construct new ones. As a consequence, observes Mori, officials in Tokyo neglected to push local governments to meet the need for new grave space. Instead, they relinquished responsibility to Buddhist temples, who, in the name of "religious freedom," teamed up with gravestone makers and real estate agents to build suburban, for-profit "soul parks" dedicated not to parishioners but to anyone willing to pay huge sums of money for the privilege of being buried in them.

Mori appeals to the state to provide for the welfare of the dead. Other critics seek change not through government but around it. Members of the Sōsō no Jiyū o Susumerukai (Society for the Promotion of Funereal Freedom) argue that Japanese should escape the grave altogether and opt instead for the scattering of cremated remains (*sankotsu*), which their society promotes as more environmentally friendly than building graveyards. Unlike Mori, they reject the regulatory power of the state, arguing that Japanese should be free to scatter remains where they please, whether on land or at sea. In addition to making an environmental argument, supporters of scattering stress that the practice frees women from patriarchal graves.

Social Networking in Death

Yet among those women who challenge convention—and their numbers are on the rise—very few choose the option of scattering. Most unmarried women, as well as married women seeking what amounts to posthumous divorce, do not want to leave society altogether when they die. Instead, they want to choose the particular society they wish to keep. Thus many decide to be buried with their natal families instead of their families of marriage. Japan has also seen an increase in recent years in the construction of shared graves for those either excluded from, or opting out of, the family system. A particularly famous example is a tomb established in 1990 at a temple in Kyoto for the Onna no Iwabuminokai (Society of the Gravestone for Women), a group composed of elderly women who had not been able to marry when they were young primarily because so many men had been killed during the war. Periodic festivals and memorial services held at the tomb bring together these women while they are still alive, helping them to form the social networks that they wish for in death.

Care for the society's tomb is entrusted to Buddhist priests, demonstrating that challenging one convention often entails supporting another. Indeed, the profusion of literature promoting or discussing alternative death rites disguises the fact that the vast majority of Japanese continue to opt for the familiar rather than the new. Even those who want to break free from established patterns often find, like their ancestors, that they cannot. In *Ima sōgi, ohaka ga kawaru* (Funerals and graves today are changing), author Inoue Haruo relates the story of a woman whose husband died of cancer in the hospital. He had repeatedly pleaded with his wife to take him home, but there was no way to care for him there. He died in the hospital against his wishes. Because he was "very independent-minded" while alive, the husband had also told his wife how he wanted to be memorialized. He did not want the usual funeral, since he hated sutra reading, he said. Instead, he asked for a simple ceremony with pleasant music. Yet in this respect too, the will of the dead was frustrated because the wife had to consider the convenience of the survivors. It was especially important to think of their son's business relations, she explained, so the social pressure compelled her to go ahead with a standard Japanese funeral.

What does the future hold for death rites in Japan? History shows that one thing is certain: whatever the changes, the dead will remain at the mercy of the living, and so too will the living remain hostage to the dead.

> *"Pre-funerals . . . bring to light the image of a person who is self-assured and has lived in the company of others, but is now allowed to more freely follow personal pleasure."*

Pre-funerals in Contemporary Japan

Satsuki Kawano

Satsuki Kawano is an anthropologist in the Department of Sociology and Anthropology at the University of Guelph in Ontario, Canada. She previously taught at Harvard University and the University of Notre Dame. As a postdoctoral fellow with the Social Science Research Council–Japan Society for the Promotion of Science, she visited Waseda University in Tokyo to conduct a research project on changing death and memorial rites in contemporary Japan. The following viewpoint describes the relatively new ceremony seizenso, *a "pre-funeral" or "living funeral" conducted by a person for him- or herself while still alive.*

As you read, consider the following questions:

1. Why do older people in Japan plan pre-funerals for themselves?

Satsuki Kawano, "Pre-Funerals in Contemporary Japan: The Making of a New Ceremony of Later Life Among Aging Japanese," *Ethnology*, vol. 43, no. 2, Spring 2004, pp. 155–165. Copyright © 2004 by the University of Pittsburgh. All rights reserved. Reproduced by permission.

2. In what ways are pre-funerals similar to tradition (post-death) funerals?

3. Why does the author of the viewpoint compare pre-funerals to wedding banquets?

The development of contemporary pre-funerals during the early 1990s is best understood by considering the influence of commercialized mortuary practices in Japan. By the late 1980s, funerals had become packaged ceremonies for mass consumption. With urbanization and the weakening of community ties, the funeral industry came to dominate the production of mortuary ceremonies. Funeral specialists are said to have pressured the bereaved to buy packaged funerals without allowing them to consider cost and need. In response to the funeral industry's dominance, there was increasing disgust with the loss of personal control and meaning in mortuary ceremonies, and during the 1990s people began to reclaim some control in mortuary practices. Deploring the commercialization of death, voices arose demanding clearer pricing policies, broader service choices, and customized package deals. People began to create their own ceremonies. The planners of pre-funerals examined in this study share these characteristics to different degrees, but are alike in determining to stage their endings in personally meaningful ways. Some explicitly stated that they were dissatisfied with their kin's funerals. Actress Mizunoe Takiko, for example, decided to hold a pre-funeral because she was unhappy with her sister's routinized funeral (*jimuteki*).

Those choosing to have a pre-funeral challenge a common assumption that survivors take charge of mortuary arrangements. The pre-funeral does not replace a regular funeral, yet planners of pre-funerals indicate their desire to take charge of their mortuary ceremonies and say that they do not need a regular funeral. The idea of the pre-funeral resonates with an emerging trend in regular funerals emphasizing self-planning, customization, and personalization. A growing number of older persons today make funeral plans by contracting with a funeral specialist or by communicating with the family. Yet with the pre-funeral the deceased-to-be takes the lead in executing the plan, playing the central role during the ceremony, and interacting directly with guests. In sum, the pre-funeral allows the individual to plan and enjoy the occasion as the designer, director, actor, and spectator.

Although performers of pre-funerals are critical of regular funerals, this alone does not move them to plan pre-funerals. They are led to consider doing so partly by some event reminding them that they are old and not immortal. Performers of pre-funerals say their experiences with death made them realize how temporary their existence is, and they found pre-funerals suitable vehicles for their feelings. One 80-year-old man from Osaka stated that a dream about death encouraged him to plan a pre-funeral. Their encounters with death or near-death become more acute through illness, surgeries, and the deaths of friends and kin. A 73-year-old man, for example, reported that his cancer surgery five years previously prompted him to consider holding a pre-funeral. The youngest person in the sample reported that he was misdiagnosed with cancer when he was in his fifties and held his pre-funeral with the thought that he was to die soon. Few people, however, were or thought they were terminally ill when they held pre-funerals.

Emphasizing the pre-funeral's practical value, its supporters say they reduce stress on families. A full-fledged funeral strains survivors emotionally and financially. An informant in her late sixties said, "Funerals consume survivors, and my older sister became bedridden for several months after holding the funeral for her deceased husband." With a regular funeral, the bereaved must make many decisions, and problems easily develop because the occasion involves a variety of people; religious specialists, funeral specialists, helpers, guests, and kin. Funeral specialists might try forcing an expensive package on clients, relatives might fight over arrangements for guests, or the bereaved might know too little about the deceased's social relations to make informed decisions. A man in his forties declared. "In my hometown, you become a full-grown adult only after successfully managing a full-fledged funeral." Financial issues, moreover, increase the stress placed on the bereaved. According to a municipal survey, the average cost of a funeral in Tokyo was 3,810,000 yen (approximately US$32,000). Even though the deceased might have saved money for the funeral, it can still cost the bereaved a small fortune. . . .

Pre-funerals resemble regular funerals in many ways. Typically, family members and friends attend pre-funerals, which take place at hotels and community halls. The size of a pre-funeral varies; those examined in this study ranged from 60 to 500 guests. The ceremonial altar, often decorated with flowers, accommodates the deceased-to-be's portrait. Guests offer flowers at the altar, give speeches to honor the deceased-to-be, and share food and drinks.

Pre-funerals highlight the theme of social parting, prevailing in regular funerals, while downplaying the religious tone. A contemporary funeral typically consists of a death ritual (*sôgi*) and a farewell ceremony (*kokubetsushiki*), which provides an occasion for the living to part with the deceased. Usually a religious specialist (most commonly a Buddhist priest) performs a ritual making the deceased a disciple of Buddha and sending the soul to a Buddhist paradise. Although most funerals are conducted with Buddhist religious elements, people are more likely to define funerals in social terms. According to the 1995 municipal survey conducted in Tokyo, 60 per cent of the respondents said the funeral is "a customary occasion for parting with the deceased," while some 30 per cent stated it is "a religious occasion to pray for the peaceful rest of the deceased."

Pre-death funerals amplify the element of parting. Aware that health in old age is a gift, performers send farewell greetings to those around them. At the same time, they express gratitude to participants, which is a job of the bereaved at a regular funeral. Thus the pre-funeral goes beyond the regular funeral by allowing the deceased-to-be to communicate with the guests in person. A 69-year-old widow in Tokyo stated: "My grandchild said it's strange to have a funeral for a living person. I said I'd like to see and thank people to whom I am indebted while I am still healthy."

Despite the element of parting that links the regular and pre-funeral, they differ in several ways. The pre-funeral less commonly involves a religious specialist chanting Buddhist sutras. Instead, an amateur or professional musical performance accompanies pre-funerals. In one case, a guest sang a song he wrote for the deceased-to-be. In addition, planners of the pre-funeral sometimes dress in festive costume instead of traditional funeral dress. The pre-funeral, therefore, dramatizes social parting more than a religious rite. A lack of strict commitment to Buddhist funeral conventions is not surprising, considering that the performers often find conventional funerals unsatisfactory. Although the bereaved usually receive incense money and pay for a significant portion of funeral expenses, guests at some pre-funerals paid a small flat fee such as 3,000 or 5,000 yen. a practice common for Japanese banquets.

In staging a social parting, pre-funerals employ a range of activities making the deceased-to-be the center of attention. Guests give speeches praising the celebrant, for example, rather than expressing sympathy to survivors. Video and slide presentations might offer additional commentary on the person's life. In some cases the deceased-to-be performs, playing music or singing karaoke. These practices make pre-funerals resemble wedding banquets. Everyone is said to be the center of attention at least once in life—at his or her wedding. The pre-funeral, however, provides a second chance in later life, which its performers enjoy. A funeral co-ordinator pointed out,

"There is a regret that the deceased, the central figure of the funeral, can't say anything to those who gathered." The pre-funeral is considered a solution to this problem. . . .

The pre-funeral's ideas of independence and departure from social duties go well beyond those of Japanese personhood that pervade anthropological writings. Rather than fostering separateness and independence, the ideology of personhood in Japan promotes mutual dependence. This ideal permeates every facet of life in Japan: socialization, schooling, work, and family. A great deal of energy is spent on making a child sensitive to the social nature of personhood. The idea that a person lives by others' support is also evident in the cultural construction of ritual. Older persons in northern Japan daily engage in sports, games, and social activities in an attempt to prevent falling into the condition of senility (*boke*), a form of social death making a person helplessly dependent on others for care. Once trapped, senile persons have no control over their dissociate states. In pre-funerals, older Japanese persons idealize a kind of dissociation whose degree and scale they control with the aim of truly enjoying the remainder of their life.

Pre-funerals offer an age-specific, alternative ideal of personhood in later life. They bring to light the image of a person who is self-assured and has lived in the company of others, but is now allowed to more freely follow personal pleasure. For a younger person, focusing on oneself creates a negative impression of self-centeredness. Unlike a young person who might not yet have learned proper social skills, the deceased-to-be in a pre-funeral is granted the presumption of having amply practiced interdependence. In fact, far from denying the importance of mutuality and support from others, pre-funerals are used to express gratitude for the support from family, friends, and relations. . . .

Pre-funerals constitute a ceremonial response to Japan's aging society, where longevity is no longer a gift but a social

burden. The age of 61 (*kanreki*) formerly marked the beginning of old age, but no longer does. If long life is a destiny
rather than a blessing, and potentially "cursed with long illness," mass longevity influences not only policy-making but
also ceremonies. Unlike official eldercare policies, pre-funerals
are shaped by old persons with their own visions of what to
do with their longevity. And their visions challenge those of
policymakers who dismiss the agency of the aging, treating
them as dependents on family and society. The users of pre-
funerals long for self-sufficiency and independence, and the
pre-funeral trumpets its users' refusal to become docile care
receivers. Older persons take charge, command attention, and
enjoy being central figures. Sometimes going against the wishes
of their children and those around them, they publicly an-
nounce egocentric orientations against cherished ideas of mutual dependence. It is worth noting that the aging examined
here grappled with conventions and created new practices.
Neither guardians of traditions nor liminal persons struggling
outside the social structure users of pre-funerals cast themselves as agents of change. . . .

In conclusion, pre-funerals are self-initiated ceremonies of
farewell and renewal in later life. In these ceremonies, older
persons take charge of their own lives, redirecting them away
from social duties. Pre-funerals celebrate powerful images of
older persons as decision-makers and consumers, as the quality of long life, rather than longevity itself, has become a central issue for the aging.

Periodical Bibliography

Economist	"Face Value: Changing How Japan Works," September 29, 2007.
Martin Fackler	"A Japanese Export: Talent," *New York Times*, May 24, 2007.
Gary Feuerberg	"Rips in Fabric of Japanese Society," *Epoch Times*, February 28, 2008. http://en.epochtimes.com.
Ilya Garger	"One Nation Under Cute: Hello Kitty, Everyman's Therapist," *Psychology Today*, March–April 2007.
Babu Gogineni	"The Buraku People of Japan," *International Humanist and Ethical Union*, December 7, 2006. www.iheu.org.
Mary Alice Hassad	"Transformation of Japan's Civil Society Landscape," *Journal of East Asia Studies*, vol. 7, 2007.
Michael Hassett	"Custody Battles: An Unfair Fight," *Japan Times*, August 12, 2008.
Miho Iwakuma	"Culture, Disability, and Disability Community: Notes on Differences and Similarities between Japan and the United States," *Atenea*, June 2005.
Donald McNeil Jr.	"Japanese Slowly Shedding Their Misgivings About the Use of Painkilling Drugs," *New York Times*, September 10, 2007.
Norimitsu Onishi	"A Japanese Maverick Wins U.S. Following," *International Herald Tribune*, June 15, 2005.
Masaki Tsubuku	"Assemblywoman Puts Sex on the Agenda: Lesbian Politician Kanako Otsuji Talks About Gender Issues in Japan," *Japan Times*, September 11, 2005.

OPPOSING
VIEWPOINTS®
SERIES

CHAPTER 4

How Does Japan Reconcile Its Past with Its Present?

Chapter Preface

Although India is the nation that is best known for its caste system, Japan had its own for hundreds of years. Social distinctions most likely predate the seventeenth century, but from 1603 to 1867—the Edo period—Japanese society was officially separated into four classes: samurai, farmers, artisans, and merchants. Laws dictated how people from the different classes interacted with each other, where they could live, what they could wear, and what professions they could adopt. Above the highest class (the samurai) were the nobles; below the lowest class were the *burakumin*.

Rules and beliefs within Shinto and Buddhism regarding killing and defilement prevented adherents from slaughtering animals or executing people, making leather, or burying the dead—essential functions in Japanese society. So the burakumin class was relegated the task of handling the tasks surrounding death and accepting defilement, which consequently made them unfit to associate with other Japanese. They were shunted as a group to the outskirts of their communities, which explains the origin of their name: *buraku* refers to small, rural neighborhoods or hamlets; *min* simply means "people." First isolated, then vilified, the burakumin experienced centuries of legalized and institutionalized discrimination and abuse, with no opportunity to change castes. The start of the Meiji era in 1868 resulted in the end of the caste system in 1869, and the government issued a decree in 1871 that gave legal rights to outcast groups. Popular attitudes, nonetheless, persisted, and the burakumin retained their low social status and continued to endure discrimination, throughout the twentieth century to today.

Despite attaining legal equality, the burakumin are easily identified by their family places of origin—many of the communities of burakumin are located in the same towns and districts that they have always been in. It was the habit until quite recently for prospective employers and marriage partners to check a person's family background; burakumin ancestry would be grounds to end the relationship. As a class, the burakumin experience more poverty and receive less education than other groups of Japanese people, despite the fact that they are physically and linguistically indistinguishable from their compatriots. Fortunately, the government has been taking steps to promote the welfare of burakumin communities and to protect the privacy of individuals; it is illegal now to run revealing background checks without permission (although individuals defy the law in some cases). With the decline and elimination of marriage discrimination, more burakumin people marry outside of the class each year, and the group will eventually assimilate into mainstream society and disappear.

Such passive efforts will succeed within generations, but the burakumin people are uniting now to demand equal treatment, too. Organizations have formed to raise awareness and speak on behalf of burakumin people—some more militant than others. Even with such openness and progress, however, parents still struggle with whether to inform their children of their burakumin identity, and the burakumin still debate how much of their plight can be changed by government and how much must be changed within themselves. Furthermore, the nation of Japan must decide as a whole whether to recognize the burakumin as a social group worthy of respect or to release individuals from the abuses of history by letting the burakumin identity fade away entirely. It was never, after all, a distinct culture.

The following chapter addresses other unhappy truths about Japanese political and social history and how the repercussions of former policies and practices continue to affect the Japanese people today.

"Most of Japan's [war] victims, including millions in China, have not received a penny. And in the small minority of cases in which compensation has been paid, the sums have been laughable."

Japan Has Not Fairly Compensated Its World War II Victims

Eamonn Fingleton

A former editor for Forbes *and the* Financial Times, *Eamonn Fingleton has been monitoring East Asian economics since 1986. He is the author of several books about global economics and the financial relationships between the United States and Asian nations. In the following viewpoint, Fingleton argues that the media and some of Japan's allies, most notably the United States, have aided Japan in hiding the fact that Japan has neglected to compensate many of its World War II victims.*

Eamonn Fingleton, "Life after Wartime," *The American Prospect*, vol. 17, April 16, 2006, pp. 41–43. Copyright © 2006 by The American Prospect, Inc. All rights reserved. Reproduced with permission from The American Prospect, 11 Beacon Street, Suite 1120, Boston, MA 02108.

As you read, consider the following questions:

1. According to Fingleton, how do payments to World War II victims of the Japanese army and government compare with payments to World War II victims of the German army and government?

2. What did the Chinese government gain by renouncing the claims of Chinese citizens to compensation by Japan, according to the author?

3. Why have most class-action lawsuits against the Japanese government regarding World War II compensation come to nothing, in Fingleton's opinion?

In all the public bickering recently between Japan and China, one fact has received remarkably little attention: Japan's continuing refusal to pay compensation to victims of its militarist-era brutality.

Ever since Japan surrendered in August 1945, one of the Japanese government's key policy objectives has been to slough off all such compensation claims. Japanese officials seem never to have discussed their argument against compensation publicly, but it would appear to amount to no more than the *sotto voce* invocation of the old saw that all's fair in love and war. Any defense lawyer taking Japan's case would no doubt argue that there was a distinction in principle between Japan's atrocities and Germany's program of mass extermination of the Jews and other minorities. (For the most part, Japan's atrocities were committed in the general pursuit of war, though this defense can hardly do much to excuse, for instance, the massacre at Nanking in 1937 or the truly gruesome activities of Unit 731, Japan's China-based biological warfare research institute.)

As best can be determined, Japan's compensation payments both to war victims and their heirs have totaled a mere $1 billion. This contrasts remarkably with Germany's record. Already by the early-1990s, Germany's payments to victims and their heirs had exceeded $70 billion. The contrast is all the more remarkable for the fact that Imperial Japan's victims outnumbered those of the Nazis by at least three to one.

The truth is that most of Japan's victims, including millions in China, have not received a penny. And in the small minority of cases in which compensation has been paid, the sums have been laughable. In the case of thousands of American servicemen who were interned in Japanese prisoner of war camps, for instance, payments have ranged between $1 and $2.50 for each day they were held. (For someone who was held for 18 months the compensation might have amounted to approximately $600 to $1,000.) Admittedly, most payments were made within a few years of the end of the war, and thus their purchasing power was considerably greater than it seems today. But even at the time, the compensation rates were only a small fraction of what, say, insurance companies in the United States or Britain would have paid to victims of industrial accidents. Yet, by all accounts, the pain and suffering experienced in Japan's prison camps were at least as serious as that suffered by a typical industrial accident victim.

Is this a fair comparison? There are, of course, few precedents in international law to guide us on these issues. What can be said is that there have long been unequivocal standards for treating prisoners of war and, in the case of hundreds of thousands of Allied troops, Japan fell brutally short of such standards. That life in Japan's prison camps was no picnic is attested to by former Veterans Administration official Charles A. Stenger, who has calculated that more than 40 percent of the 27,465 U.S. Army and Air Force personnel imprisoned in the Pacific died in detention. The equivalent figure for German prison camps was a little more than 1 percent. (These figures do not include the Navy and Marine Corps.)

Why has there not been more pressure on Tokyo to do the right thing by countless innocent victims? And why has Japan's niggardliness received so little attention in the West? Few actors emerge from this story with much glory. Not the leaders of the American occupation of postwar Japan. Not the American press. And not even the governments of the various East Asian nations whose citizens suffered disproportionately under Imperial Japan.

A Flimsy Excuse

Japan's first gambit was to plead poverty. In the immediate aftermath of World War II, this had the merit of verisimilitude. Deprived of vital raw materials previously sourced from Japan's overseas empire, Japanese industry slumped in the late 1940s and Japanese per-capita income fell below that of some sub-Saharan African nations. But anyone who took Japan's then straitened circumstances as indicative of its future prospects was lacking in foresight. Before World War II, after all, Japan had ranked well up among the world's richer nations. Its remarkable manufacturing prowess was already becoming apparent, albeit mainly in armaments. The Mitsubishi Zero, for instance, was an engineering marvel, which at the time of its launch in 1940 was the most sophisticated fighter plane in the world.

Yet by the late 1940s, Japanese leaders had convinced American officials that Japan would never again be an advanced economy. The common wisdom of the time was that Japan's export efforts would be focused on the Third World markets and would consist mainly of supplying cheap "knick-knacks"—a word used in at least one official American economic analysis of the time.

It was in this atmosphere that an American mission visited Japan in 1948 to guide Washington on the reparations question. The so-called Draper-Johnson mission more or less absolved Japan of all liabilities. There have been allegations that some of the mission's members had serious conflicts of interest because they represented American financial organizations that had extensive pre-war dealings with Japan's so-called

A Revised History

The [Japanese] Ministry of Education ordered publishers to delete passages [about] the Battle of Okinawa [in 2007]. . .

[According to an earlier history,] Japanese soldiers . . . persuaded locals that victorious American soldiers would go on a rampage of killing and raping. With the impending victory of American troops, civilians committed mass suicide, urged on by fanatical Japanese soldiers.

"There were some people who were forced to commit suicide by the Japanese Army," one old textbook explained. But in the revision ordered by the ministry, it now reads, "There were some people who were driven to mass suicide."

Norimitsu Onishi,
New York Times, *April 1, 2007.*

zaibatsus, which were the industrial groupings that dominated the Japanese economy in the first half of the 20th century. Not the least of the conflicts appears to have concerned Army Undersecretary William H. Draper Jr., who was the mission's effective leader. Dillon, Read & Co., the investment banking firm where Draper had worked before the war and where he returned after the war, received a lucrative Japanese underwriting deal soon after the mission reported.

In the words of one observer, it was as if the foxes had been sent to inventory the henhouse.

Serving Government Interests

The Draper-Johnson mission's key recommendations were incorporated into the Treaty of San Francisco in 1951. Signed by the United States, Japan, and more than 40 other nations, this document formally sealed all issues arising out of the war. It was, however, a case of Hamlet without the prince. For one key nation was not a signatory—China, which of course was home to by far the largest group of potential claimants for compensation. When China began opening up in the 1970s, one of Tokyo's first moves was to press Zhou Enlai, China's Japan-educated foreign minister, to renounce the Chinese people's claims to compensation. For reasons that have never been made clear, he duly did so. His renunciation was endorsed by the reformist regime of Deng Xiaoping in the late 1970s, but in this case there was a quid pro quo: Japan promised to favor China in its foreign-aid program.

While this did essentially nothing for the victims, it represented a win-win for both the Chinese and Japanese governments. Chinese officials got to designate the projects on which Japan's money would be spent. Meanwhile for Tokyo, the cost of the aid program—a cumulative total of about $30 billion—was a mere bagatelle compared to what would have been payable had Japan been forced to negotiate with millions of individual Chinese claimants in the world's courts. The aid program, moreover, was a source of countless lucrative contracts for major Japanese manufacturers that supply most of the bulldozers, electricity generating sets, and countless other types of capital equipment used in Japan's China aid program.

Media Spin and Lies of Omission

Perhaps the most remarkable aspect of the whole story is how it has been played in the English-language press. The tone has been set by *The Japan Times*, a Tokyo-based English-language newspaper long regarded as a semi-official mouthpiece of the Japanese Foreign Ministry. The *Times* has generally avoided the subject of compensation and instead has assiduously encouraged Westerners to see the war legacy story as merely a question of whether Japan has apologized sincerely enough. It has repeatedly led the foreign press in bouts of parsing Japan's words of apology. Its approach has been echoed by the Japanese establishment's many surrogates and stooges in the Tokyo foreign community, and foreign correspondents seem to buy into the gambit, getting too engrossed in semantics to ask about compensation.

The semantics-only approach remained the status quo until 1997, when Iris Chang published a best-selling account of the Nanking massacre. The book's comments on the compensation issue finally precipitated what Tokyo had long feared: a flood of class-action lawsuits in American courts. Her role was catalytic: the main effect of her book was to bring to the attention of a younger generation of class-action lawyers that Japan had never compensated most WWII victims.

The lawyers arrived too late, however: Most would-be claimants were already dead, and much evidence had disappeared. Moreover, much of what evidence does exist is held either by the Japanese government or by Japanese corporations, which have refused to release it. As Tokyo had hoped, justice delayed proved to be justice denied. Still, thereafter the curfew on compensation talk was moot, and even the most timid members of the Tokyo press community came out on the issue. Some even went so far as to discuss the previously ultra-taboo issue of the German/Japanese dichotomy on compensation.

Virtually every correspondent who ever covered Tokyo bears some responsibility for the press's monumental blind spot. But few have been guilty of a greater lapse than the Anglo-Dutch writer Ian Buruma. In 1994, Buruma, a former writer for *The Japan Times*, published *The Wages of Guilt*, a book contrasting Japanese and German war legacies. Although the jacket promised "devastating truths," one devastating truth went unrecorded: the startling difference in the two nations' compensation records. Questioned at a public meeting in Tokyo some years ago, Buruma replied that the book had mentioned the compensation issue. Buruma pointed to a single sentence referring to the fact that some victims of one little-known atrocity by the Japanese had never been compensated. He offered no explanation for the book's silence on the differing compensation policies of Japan and Germany.

Anyone familiar with Buruma's theme will notice other lacunae in *The Wages of Guilt.* In particular, the book failed to follow up on the subsequent careers of some of Japan's more notorious war criminals, particularly those in Unit 731. Not only did the United States drop war-crimes charges against the unit's personnel in return for access to Unit 731's secrets, but these personnel were never punished. Quite the contrary, many of the doctors who conducted Unit 731's most diabolic experiments went on to extraordinarily successful careers in postwar Japanese medicine. One became president of Japan's national medical association in the late 1940s—right under the nose of the American occupation.

A Failure to Reciprocate

For Americans, perhaps the most galling aspect of the Japanese failures on reparations is the contrast between the tight-fistedness toward war victims displayed by the Japanese government and the generosity with which the U.S. government treated postwar Japan. According to a 1970 edition of *Encyclopedia Britannica,* the United States spent $2 billion on aid to Japan in the first six years after the war. This is double my estimate of Japan's total compensation payments to war victims (this estimate, which I published in a book in 1995, came from Leon Hollerman, an economist who served in the U.S. occupation of Japan in the late 1940s).

To say the least, the compensation story casts the recent spats between Tokyo and Beijing in a different light. It is hard to say which side is more cynical. The only reason Japanese voters are not more outraged by Prime Minister Junichiro Koizumi's baiting of Beijing is that they know so little of the depth of the Chinese people's grievances. The Japanese press, after all, has printed only a very selective account of the past. By the same token, those in the Beijing leadership who have sought to whip up popular anger against Tokyo are the same people who have systematically done Tokyo's bidding by blocking Chinese citizens from suing the Japanese government in American courts.

> *"The [Japanese] government has recog-*
> *nized [the Ainu] as an indigenous*
> *people."*

Japan Has Officially Recognized the Rights of Its Indigenous People

Mariko Sakai and Shozo Nakayama

Mariko Sakai and Shozo Nakayama are staff writers at The Daily Yomiuri *(Yomiuri Shimbun), an English-language news-paper that has the largest circulation of any newspaper in Japan. In the following viewpoint, the authors describe recent legislative changes in Japan granting the Ainu—an ethnic group that lives on the northern islands of Japan, especially Hokkaido—status as "indigenous people." Prior to this ruling, the Japanese govern-ment had not regarded the Ainu as having a culture worth pre-serving, let alone a people who belonged in Japanese society, the authors note. Despite the ruling, the authors maintain, much work still remains to be done to clarify and implement it.*

As you read, consider the following questions:

1. What statistics, as cited by the authors, demonstrate how the Ainu have fallen behind their Japanese neighbors?

Mariko Sakai and Shozo Nakayama, "Restoration of Ainu Rights Step Nearer," *The Daily Yomiuri (Japan)*, June 11, 2008, p. 4. Copyright © 2008 by The Yomiuri Shimbun. Re-produced by permission.

2. What does the United Nations Declaration on the Rights of Indigenous Peoples call for from the Japanese government, as reported by Sakai and Nakayama?

3. What is one possible reason given by the authors for why the Japanese government has not yet defined exactly what it will consider "indigenous people"?

A Diet [the Japanese parliament] resolution . . . recognizing the Ainu as indigenous to Hokkaido and neighboring parts of northern Japan has created hope that progress will be made in restoring the rights of the Ainu people.

In response to the resolution, which was approved unanimously in both chambers of the legislature [June 6, 2008], the government drew up a policy the same day to give official recognition of the indigenous status of the Ainu for the first time.

A slew of problems still need to be addressed from this point on, including how to deal with such issues as the land and natural resources the Ainu were deprived of in the process of Japan's modernization.

Tadashi Kato, chairman of the Hokkaido Utah Association, was visibly overwhelmed with emotion at a press conference in the Diet Building following the adoption of the resolution.

The Hokkaido Utari Association—Utari signifies brethren in Ainu—was formerly known as the Ainu Association of Hokkaido. This body has been working since the end of World War II to enhance the social status of the Ainu, many of whom live in Hokkaido.

"Mr. [Nobutaka] Machimura, the chief Cabinet secretary, has made it clear that the government has recognized us as an indigenous people," Kato said. "After a lapse of 140 years [since the Meiji Restoration], we can finally see some light. I can hardly find the words to fully express our gratitude."

Present Circumstances Harsh

The U.N. Declaration on the Rights of Indigenous Peoples, which was adopted by the General Assembly of the world body in September [2007], helped propel the Diet to pass the resolution.

Also conducive to Diet approval of the resolution was the government's judgment that it needed to clarify its position on the issue before the . . . Group of Eight summit meeting [an international forum for the eight most powerful nations] in July [2008] in Toyakocho, Hokkaido.

The circumstances in which the Ainu find themselves today, however, remain harsh.

According to a survey by the Hokkaido prefectural government in 2006, 23,782 Ainu live in Hokkaido. Of them, 3.8 percent were on welfare, 1.3 points higher than the average figure for welfare recipients among residents of the cities, towns and villages in which the Ainu live.

In addition, no more than 17.4 percent of Ainu received a college education, far below the average of 38.5 percent for all residents of those communities.

This state of affairs reflects a background of long-running discrimination against the Ainu.

A History of Oppression

When the Family Registry Law was enacted in 1871, in the early Meiji era (1868–1912), the government incorporated the Ainu into the nation's family registry system, designating them to fall under the category of "commoners."

By enforcing registration, the Meiji government put into state ownership most tracts of land used by the Ainu.

Furthermore, the government prohibited the Ainu from speaking in Ainu, and banned or restricted certain traditional practices, including their hunting methods and the Iomante bear festival—an important ritual in which the Ainu thank the bear deity for providing them with bearskins and meat.

A History of Discrimination

The Japanese Diet has unanimously passed a resolution pressing the Japanese government to recognise the Ainu as indigenous people. . . . "It puts an end to years of false reporting to the United Nations by the Japanese government to the effect that 'Japan has no minorities' and therefore is not practicing discrimination," says Andrew Horvat, a professor at Tokyo Keizai University. . . . "In fact, the treatment of the Ainu over the past 150 years by the Japanese majority is no different from the said history of aboriginal peoples in the U.S., Canada or Australia."

Catherine Makino, InterPress Service, June 11, 2008.

The Meiji government was relentless in pushing ahead with its policy of assimilating the Ainu.

Under the Hokkaido Former Aborigine Protection Law, which came into force in 1899, the government gave the Ainu plots of land for nothing, but with strict conditions that banned land transfers outside inheritance.

The land given to the Ainu comprised the leftovers from plots allotted to settlers from the mainland of Japan, according to the Hokkaido Utari Association. Many of the plots were unsuitable for growing crops, the association said.

In addition, discriminatory practices against the Ainu were left unredressed, including those involving marriage and employment, it noted.

In a government statement . . . , Machimura touched on these issues.

"Many Ainu people were discriminated against and forced into poverty in the process of the nation's modernization, despite the fact they were regarded in legal terms as being equal [to Japanese] as members of the nation," the top government spokesman said.

Teruki Tsunemoto, professor at Hokkaido University's Center for Ainu & Indigenous Studies, was optimistic [that] the resolution would aid the plight of the Ainu.

"[I hope] the Diet resolution and government policy pledge will serve as a catalyst for raising awareness that the Ainu issue isn't limited in significance to Hokkaido, but is a problem for the nation as a whole," Tsunemoto said.

Two Sets of Rights

Numerous problems involving how to deal with the rights of the Ainu as an indigenous people have yet to be addressed, however.

The U.N. declaration calls for the government of each country to "respect and promote the inherent rights of indigenous peoples, which derive from their political, economic and social structures and from their cultures, spiritual traditions—especially their rights to their lands, territories and resources."

Should the government accept the U.N. declaration literally, it would have to return the lands the Ainu were deprived of during the modernization process. The government also might have to grant hunting and fishing rights exclusively to the Ainu.

This would give rise to the question of how to secure consistency with the principle of equality before the law as stipulated by the Constitution.

Granting certain rights exclusively to the Ainu would run counter to the spirit of the supreme law, which guarantees rights not in terms of groups of people but in terms of each individual person.

In Canada, however, the Inuit have been given rights that are applicable only to them, plus the right to engage in whaling.

[Professor] Toshiyuki Munesue, who specializes in constitutional studies at Osaka University, said, "A system of 'dual rules in a single country' can hardly be suitable in Japan, where all segments of society have been integrated as a single nation on the basis of a single political system."

But how can the rights of the Ainu as an indigenous people be ensured without the need for a dual set of rules?

Professor emeritus Takaaki Sasaki at the National Museum of Ethnology, Osaka, said, "What's needed above all else is for Japanese as a whole to have a deeper understanding of Ainu history."

"On the basis of shared historical understanding, there should be public discussion on whether rights exclusive to the Ainu should be created," Sasaki said.

Avoiding Clear Definition

The government, in line with the Diet's Ainu resolution, plans to set up an expert panel in the Prime Minister's Office to discuss measures to be implemented for boosting the social status of the Ainu.

Machimura stated ... that the government recognizes the Ainu explicitly as an "indigenous people with their own language, culture and religion whose ancestors began to inhabit this country, mostly in the northern part of the Japanese archipelago and especially in Hokkaido, prior to the earliest ancestors of the Japanese."

The planned expert panel, if launched, will be the second of its kind.

Its predecessor, the Expert Panel on Measures for the Ainu People, was established in 1995 under the administration of then Prime Minister Tomiichi Murayama. The panel put together a report in 1996 that called for legislative action to benefit the Ainu.

The Diet subsequently enacted the existing Ainu Cultural Promotion Law in 1997, thereby abolishing the Hokkaido Former Aborigine Protection Law, which was considered a principal source of discrimination against the Ainu.

The government has so far stopped short of making any clear-cut definition of what it means by "indigenous people," on the grounds that no internationally established definition exists. But if the government is to accept the concept of indigenous peoples in line with the 2007 U.N. declaration, it could lead to possible compensation claims for land and fishing rights—a situation that could give the government a major headache.

Machimura's statement avoided any reference as to whether the government would adopt the U.N.-defined concept of indigenous peoples, and instead took the position of recognizing the Ainu as an indigenous people in a way unique to this country. The statement could be "criticized for its ambiguity," a high-ranking government official said.

The planned expert panel will be tasked with determining to what extent Japan should accept the U.N. declaration for expanding measures beneficial to the Ainu. Given that even generational gaps exist among the Ainu themselves in terms of values, the government likely has many hurdles to clear before it resolves the Ainu issue.

"As a result of globalization and rapidly changing demographics, the kimono business has collapsed, its future in question."

Some Japanese Traditions Are on the Decline

Anthony Faiola

Anthony Faiola writes for The Washington Post *about the forces of globalization, particularly its impact on the lives of people in the developing and developed worlds. In the following viewpoint, he focuses on the declining kimono industry and its last manufacturers—some of whom are more than a hundred years old. With changing tastes for Western dress and the outsourcing of kimono production, the surrounding traditions are adapting to Japan's globalized condition as well, the author points out.*

As you read, consider the following questions:

1. In what way do the changing demographics of the Japanese people contribute to the decline of the kimono industry, in Faiola's view?

2. Why does the author say the teenage-Goth-geisha fashion signals hope to many kimono manufacturers?

Anthony Faiola, "Twilight for the Kimono," *The Washington Post*, December 13, 2006, p. A23. Copyright © 2006, The Washington Post. Reprinted with permission.

3. Why have so many stages in the kimono manufacturing process been outsourced to China, according to Faiola?

Since 794, when the imperial court arrived illustriously in the new capital of Kyoto, [the kimono district of] Nishijin has clothed emperors and shoguns, princesses and geisha, prime ministers and mistresses. It survived fires and floods, the post–World War II American occupation and, for decades more, fickle tastes. Twenty-five years ago, production of Nishijin kimonos and obi—elaborate kimono sashes—was thriving, with highflying Tokyo businessmen purchasing $25,000 kimonos for wives and lovers like so many boxes of roses.

But today, as a result of globalization and rapidly changing demographics, the kimono business has collapsed, its future in question. Sales are expected to sink to an all-time low [in 2006], even as Japan has emerged from recession to experience its longest economic boom since World War II.

The prosperity has come with an altered set of cultural values. This is a country of manga comics and glittering animation. The rising moguls driving the new economy are more likely to buy muscled chrome from one of Tokyo's expanding list of Ferrari dealerships than drop their spoils on Kyoto silk.

As the kimono becomes more museum piece than couture item, what once made it quintessentially Japanese is gradually fading. Market realities have forced kimono makers to eschew expensive Japanese silk. As a result, more than 90 percent of new kimonos and obi made in Japan, including most of those from Nishijin's most venerable textile houses, are now woven from cheaper imported silk.

Like blue jeans in America, kimonos increasingly are not being made in Japan at all. In search of cut-rate labor, a growing number of ancient Japanese kimono houses have opened weaving factories in China. As the work drops off, younger Japanese craftsmen have deserted the industry in droves, leaving the last generation of masters with few heirs.

In Nishijin, the graying [102-year-old Yasujiro] Yamaguchi is one of only three masters left who can create a kimono from scratch—both conceptualizing and weaving with his own seasoned hands to infuse a garment with the intended wearer's personality. All three are over 70. None has an apprentice.

"It is a sign of the times," Yamaguchi said. "I am not sure who will carry on this tradition for future generations. I no longer have the time or energy to teach someone now. Even if I did, where would they work?"

A Wilting Industry

Few garments are as tied to a nation as the kimono is to Japan. In a society that values the unspoken, its colors and patterns have for centuries served as an alternative form of speech. Without uttering a word, a well-chosen kimono can speak volumes about a wearer's sorrow or joy, animosity or amorousness. Restricting the legs to doll-like steps, the kimono changes the way both sexes walk, making even the clumsiest appear elegant. It is essential to the classical arts of Kabuki and Noh theater, the tea ceremony and ikebana, or flower arranging. In Murasaki Shikibu's 11th-century literary masterpiece *The Tale of Genji*, gifts of kimonos in scented silk are extensions of a romancing prince's spirit. The kimono is less a garment than a window into the Japanese soul.

Although a growing taste for Western clothing washed ashore more than a century ago, the kimono long remained the vanity garment of choice for major events in Japanese life. But now, the country's own demographics are working against it.

Fewer Japanese are marrying today than ever, and those who do largely shun traditional white wedding kimonos in favor of Western-style dresses. A declining birthrate, meanwhile, has meant fewer babies, which in turn has meant fewer sales of kimonos for children's coming-of-age rites. Nationwide, kimono sales have more than halved in the past decade.

Nowhere has the decline been felt more keenly than in Nishijin, home of Japan's finest—and priciest—kimonos and obi. Sales of Nishijin products fell from $2.7 billion in 1990 to a record low of $477 million [in 2005], according to industry figures; during the same period, the district's production of kimonos dropped from 291,000 to just 87,382 garments.

At the same time, the ancient textile houses of Nishijin have fallen like cherry blossoms in late April. In 1980, there were about 1,200 kimono and obi factories and related businesses lining these ancient stone streets. Today, there are 606.

Once a lofty, ceremonious enterprise, even kimono-selling has been tainted by scandal in recent years, with desperate dealers pressuring retirees into taking out high-interest loans to buy exorbitantly priced kimonos. Faced with such accusations, the president of Azekura, a once-venerable dealer of Nishijin kimonos, committed suicide . . . by jumping from the eighth floor of a Kyoto hotel. Other establishments have faded less dramatically, through bankruptcy filings and shuttered doors.

Some see a light for the industry in the unlikeliest of places—Tokyo's hyper-hip Harajuku district, where Goth geisha in punk makeup and secondhand black kimonos strut the streets flaunting attitude and skull-faced leather purses.

"Right now, they are wearing cheap, used kimonos they bought for a few dollars in a bargain bin," said Toshimitsu Ikariyama, president of the Nishijin Textile Industrial Association. "But when these teenagers grow up and become prosperous, we hope they will be the start of a new generation who will wear more expensive and new kimonos for grace and beauty, the way their mothers and grandmothers did." . . .

A Failing Culinary Tradition

Tochi, a large-leafed deciduous tree, can grow as tall as 30 meters. The culture of eating tochi seeds is said to have existed in Japan since the Jomon period (14000–4000 BC). . . .

The custom of eating tochi quickly began to decline between the mid-1950s and mid-1960s. One of the major reasons for the decline is that tochi trees were cut down to make room to plant fast-growing Japanese cedar trees. The other reason is a change in diet; easy-to-prepare food is now widely available, whereas tochi seeds require almost a month of preprocessing. And perhaps the most worrying reason is that people who have tochi-processing skills are aging.

To eat tochi seeds, they must be soaked in a clear stream for days and treated with wood ash in order to take out the harshness of the taste. Every region is similarly challenged with the difficulty of obtaining the ash needed for this ancient process.

Natsu Shimamura,
Rediscovering the Treasures of Food,
Tokyo Foundation, 2008.

Outsourcing Kimonos to China

One hundred percent Japanese kimonos are almost impossible to find anymore. In the 1990s, Japan's troubled textile industry successfully lobbied the government to embrace globalization by opening the long-protected domestic silk industry to foreign competition. With its higher cost structure, Japanese silk thread, although considered extremely fine, is at least 20 times the average price of Chinese, Brazilian or Southeast Asian silk. As tariffs dropped and cheaper imports became widely available, the Japanese silk industry collapsed, leaving only two small factories to produce tiny quantities of inaccessibly priced thread.

"I am making kimonos more cheaply, but they are not cheap kimonos," [manufacturer Yasuto] Kawamura said. His best Chinese-made obi sell for an average of $8,000, about the same as obi made in Japan. "It was only the Japanese silk companies that said Chinese silk wasn't good."

"The kimono is not just about our country," he added. "It is about the Japanese race—our daily rituals, our history, our religion, about who we are as a people. We have to do anything we can to protect the kimono, even if that means making them overseas." . . .

Yamaguchi's small wooden workshop sits on a quiet street in Nishijin. But there was a time not so long ago when the world outside was filled with the colors now lighting up his dining table.

"The women, and men too, would come to Nishijin in kimonos to order more kimonos," he said. "The color! They would fill the streets with their color, and leave so much cash that we used rulers to count the stacks of yen because it was faster that way. Those were the days when the sounds of working looms were everywhere"

He grew quiet, glancing out his window. "But now, Nishijin is gray."

Many kimono makers who were once regarded as legends have left the business. Yamaguchi's brother, Itaro, who turns 105 on Dec. 18 [2006], spent his younger days as one of the district's most formidable kimono entrepreneurs. But he handed off his business to his eldest son, who has also largely shifted production to China. Itaro now spends his days obsessively working with local weavers on a remarkable re-creation in silk of four original *Table of Genji* scrolls.

"I wanted to leave something for future generations to see," he said, one of the extraordinarily detailed scrolls unfurled at his home, a few minutes from Nishijin. "I just want to show them what we were capable of."

Only a few blocks from Yasujiro Yamaguchi's workshop in the heart of Nishijin, more and more stores selling Western-style wedding dresses have popped up in recent years. Yamaguchi himself came face to face with changing tastes when one of his own granddaughters wore a Western dress at her wedding reception instead of an uchikake, or traditional bridal kimono.

"It cannot be helped." he said. "All we can do now is keep trying to make kimonos so beautiful that they will no longer be able to resist it. What choice do we have?"

"The recent surge in teenage girls hoping to enter the 'floating world' of [gei-
sha] is evidence of renewed respect
among the Japanese for their traditional culture."

Renewed Respect as Geisha Make a Comeback—and Take to Cyberspace

Justin McCurry

Justin McCurry is the Tokyo correspondent for the Guardian, *a
British newspaper. In the following viewpoint, McCurry describes the recent surge of interest in the "floating world" of the
geisha. Icons of traditional Japanese culture, geisha are women
highly skilled in fine arts, ceremonial rituals, and conversation,
who make appearances as musicians, dancers, or social entertainers; they are not prostitutes or escorts, the author asserts.
Training to become a geisha takes years, and working as a geisha
is arduous, albeit rewarding, McCurry explains. After almost a
century of declining numbers, women are once again perceiving
geisha to be a legitimate, desirable profession, he reports.*

Justin McCurry, "Renewed Respect as Geishas Make a Comeback—And Take to Cyberspace," *The Guardian (UK)*, June 25, 2008, p. 23. Copyright © 2008 by Guardian Newspapers Limited. Reproduced by permission of Guardian News Service, LTD.

As you read, consider the following questions:

1. What is a *maiko*, as described by McCurry?
2. What aspects of the popular culture have contributed to the recent interest in geisha, in the author's opinion?
3. What position is Miehina expected to accept someday at the Harutomi tea house, as reported by McCurry?

Miehina has barely taken a dozen steps along a Kyoto street before the audio backdrop to her every public move comes to life. In the fading light of an early summer evening, the metronomic clip-clop of her platform okobo sandals is accompanied by the clicking of shutters, as a gaggle of amateur photographers seeks the perfect snapshot of one of Japan's most venerated women.

They stay with her until she retreats down a backstreet and slips through the sliding wooden door of her teahouse, her emerald green kimono, worth tens of thousands of pounds, now no more than a photogenic imprint.

In the past tourists would have had to wait hours for a fleeting glimpse of a lone geisha on her way to an appointment. Now they are spoiled for choice.

After decades of decline, Japan's traditional entertainers are making a comeback. Earlier this year the number of geisha trainees—known as maiko—reached 100 in Kyoto for the first time in four decades.

The ancient capital is still a long way from returning to its 1920s' heyday, when there were around 800 geisha in Gion, its most famous geisha district.

In 1965, records show, the city was home to 76 maiko. By 1978, the number had fallen to 28; the number then stuck between 50 and 80.

Experts believe the recent surge in teenage girls hoping to enter the "floating world" of tea ceremonies, performing arts, and yes, flirtatious exchanges with inebriated clients, is evidence of renewed respect among the Japanese for their traditional culture.

"I remember years ago being told by one woman: 'How would the English like it if their country was represented by what many people regard as prostitutes in national dress?'" says Lesley Downer, author of Geisha: The Secret History of a Vanishing World, who lived among geisha for six months while researching her book. "The Japanese are far less concerned about appearing western than they once were. They used to be paranoid about what the west thought of them. That was particularly true of geisha, which even Japanese considered too olde-worlde."

Much of the mild embarrassment many Japanese felt about the geisha thread running through their cultural fabric arose from popular misconceptions: the suspicion that, beneath the veneer of cultural exclusivity, they were little more than high-class prostitutes.

Though illicit sex is not unheard of, the myths surrounding the geisha are slowly unravelling amid unprecedented media exposure and a belated embrace of the internet among the teahouses of Kyoto's five geisha districts.

Though it was as aesthetically removed from geisha life as Hollywood is physically from Kyoto, the 2005 film adaptation of Arthur Golden's bestseller Memoirs of a Geisha piqued interest in the profession among teenagers. Hanaikusa, a TV drama based on the autobiography of Mineko Iwasaki, the source for much of Golden's book, was one of the small-screen hits of last year.

Then came the emergence of the cyber-geisha, who combine daily study of the traditional arts with a few minutes spent on their laptops. Though free of gossip—protocol precludes any mention of clients' names or how they behave—the most popular blogs draw thousands of visitors a month, eager to soak up even the most pedestrian accounts of the maiko's working day.

"The old geisha were terribly snooty and couldn't care less what people thought of them," says Downer, who attributes teahouse websites and online maiko application forms partly to enlightened self-interest.

"Now there is more interest in presenting an image to the world that brings them bigger dividends. They finally started to worry that geisha traditions would die out, and that they needed to do something about it."

Dividends

Whether the new approach succeeds will depend on apprentices such as Miehina, now ensconced behind the bar at Harutomi, her teahouse and living quarters in Miyagawacho district.

"It wasn't that I didn't want to become a maiko," she says in her lilting Kyoto dialect as she pours beer into tiny, wafer-thin glasses. "I just didn't think I could. I wasn't mentally prepared for all the training involved."

Now 20, with three years of training behind her, she has just a few months to wait until full geisha-hood beckons. Though her talent for dancing was apparent early on, she resisted several approaches from Kyoto teahouses, relenting only when her father gave his blessing. "I knew that if I were to become part of this world, life would be totally different than it is for other teenage girls," she says.

Though she rarely sees her family and has lost touch with her school friends, she does not regret her decision. "It may appear a tough lifestyle to outsiders, but you quickly get used to the strange rhythm of maiko life. There are people looking out for you all the time. When they complain, it is because they want to make me better at what I do."

As Harutomi's only resident maiko, she will one day run the teahouse and nurture a new generation.

"This profession is about quality, not quantity," says the teahouse's owner Haruno, a retired geisha. "I'm pleased that more girls are interested in becoming geisha, but they must be up to the job. As long as they come here with the right intentions, I'm happy."

It is clear that expectations are high for the once-reluctant teenager who, her regular clients say, has become one of Miyagawacho's finest dancers.

"She is the face of Harutomi, and one day she will be in charge here," says Haruno. "If she messes up she will bring shame not only on herself, but on the teahouse . . . and her profession."

The Apprentice

After waking at 8.30, Miehina eats a light breakfast and reads the newspapers: some clients discuss current affairs. She spends the next few hours learning the three-stringed shamisen and other instruments, song and dance, the tea ceremony and the art of polite conversation. After lunch with her teahouse "mother", it is time to prepare for the evening. After applying makeup, which can take an hour, she crosses the street to be wrapped, layer by layer, in a kimono that along with hair ornaments and other accoutrements weighs several kilograms. Her appointments begin at 6pm. If at another teahouse, she must be back at Harutomi by midnight. She rarely sleeps before 3am. Her days off are the second and fourth Sundays.

Periodical Bibliography

Hannah Beech "Japan's New Groove," *Time International* (Asia Edition), August 25, 2008.

Joseph Coleman "60 Years Later, Japan's Remorse over World War II Is Still a Matter of Debate," *Associated Press*, July 30, 2005. www.ap.org.

John Dodd "A Marriage Maestro Wed to Innovation: Masahiro Hirose Has Successfully Customized Nuptials to Revive the Wedding Industry," *Japan Inc.*, January 2005.

Robert Fulford "Guilt, Identity, and Japaneseness," *Queen's Quarterly*, Fall 2006.

Ayako Karino "Endangered Species: Silent-Film Narrators Passionate About Their Work," *International Herald Tribune/Asahi Weekly*, March 5, 2005.

Leo Lewis "Japan Hopes to Turn Sci-Fi into Reality with Elevator to the Stars," *Times Online* (London), September 22, 2008. www.timesonline.co.uk.

Tessa Morris-Suzuki "Japan's 'Comfort Women': It's Time for the Truth," *Japan Focus*, March 8, 2007. www.japanfocus.org.

Rebecca Palmer "Reviving a Taste of Tradition in Japan's 'Rice Kingdom,'" *Dominion Post* (New Zealand), November 3, 2008.

Bennett Richardson "After 26 Centuries, Is Japan Finally Fit for a Queen?" *Christian Science Monitor*, July 28, 2005.

Daiki Shibuichi "Japan's History Textbook Controversy," *Electronic Journal of Contemporary Japanese Studies*, March 4, 2008. www.japanesestudies.co.uk.

Akiko Takeyama "Beauty of Seduction in a Tokyo Host Club," *IIAS Newsletter*, Spring 2006. www.iias.nl.

For Further Discussion

Chapter 1

1. A nation's fertility rate usually depends on the fertility of its women because women bear the children. Programs to encourage fertility, therefore, focus on women's choices of how many children to have. Accordingly, Japanese government policies emphasize that it is women who can make a difference. Is this fair? Are individual women responsible for conceiving and bearing the children of the next generation? Should fertility be a government concern at all? Why or why not?

2. Women in nearly every nation have been fighting for decades (sometimes centuries) for rights equal to men, and they have made significant strides in most modern societies. Should the Japanese government do more to promote the rights of women? Can proactive efforts to establish the perception that women are equal to men shorten the length of time required for gender attitudes to transform? Why or why not? Cite from the viewpoints in framing your answer.

3. Japan's impending population crisis has not only an economic impact but also a cultural one. Not enough babies are being born to work or to learn (and transmit to subsequent generations) Japanese traditions and language. Opening the borders to immigrants and loosening requirements for citizenship may solve the labor problem, but many people fear that the Japanese culture would be diluted or disappear altogether. Do you think this fear is reasonable? Can immigrant cultures affect the dominant culture significantly? How do you think the Japanese cul-

ture would affect immigrants' culture? Consider short-term and multigeneration effects in your answer, citing from the viewpoints.

Chapter 2

1. Japanese car and electronics companies perform very well internationally; Japanese entertainment products are wildly popular worldwide, but Japan's entertainment companies do not make a proportional amount of profit. Roland Kelts argues that Japanese business culture is unsure about how to handle intellectual property (versus tangible goods). What other factors—such as digital media and file-sharing systems—might contribute to the economic success or failure of a company producing movies and animation?

2. Japan is not the only country hunting whales for food. Norway is openly engaged in commercial whale hunting, and Japan claims simultaneously that whale hunting for food is part of its cultural heritage and that whale meat is a by-product of whales killed for scientific study. Both of those Japanese claims are widely contested, and Japan seems to be singled out in the popular culture and media for vilification, at least in the United States. What are some reasons that might contribute to the particularly negative portrayal of Japan in this matter? Is geographical proximity to the United States a factor? Is racism? Is Japan a less trustworthy nation than Norway? To what degree do nations have the right to intervene in another country's hunting habits? Explain your answers, citing from the viewpoints.

Chapter 3

1. Veronica Chambers presents Japan as a fruitful place for enterprising women and mothers while the *Economist* paints a picture of Japan that stifles men who have ideas

for businesses outside the usual corporate culture. To what extent does gender affect the perception of entrepreneurs? Are women's businesses judged differently than men's businesses? Does a failed business make a woman a "failure" in the same way it may make a man one? Suggest some reasons that male and female entrepreneurs might experience different levels of economic, professional, and personal risk, or why launching a new business is risky in the same way no matter who does it.

2. Japan is worried about the health of its older citizens for a variety of reasons, including financial ones. Is measuring the waistlines of its citizens and penalizing them for exceeding a weight range a justified exercise of government power? The government is the primary health care provider of the people; does any agency that pays for health care have the right to penalize recipients of care for not maintaining minimum standards of health? Consider that Japanese people cannot easily switch to another competing insurance company, but that they can vote for the government officials who make such decisions. Is obesity justifiably classed as a public health issue or is it realistically only a personal problem? Explain your answers.

3. It is said that funerals are for the living, and the traditional funeral rites (and expenses) in Japan certainly seem to support that statement. Given the social importance of a correct funeral in Japan, is staging your own funeral (while you are alive) before your descendants can host one for you (after you die) considerate or selfish? On the other hand, is it culturally beneficial for a society to honor ancient practices and tradition with elaborate funerals even if it means denying the wishes of the person who has died? Explain your answers, citing from the viewpoints and your own experience.

Chapter 4

1. Japan often is criticized for whitewashing its history, sometimes to the point of denying unpleasant realities. Why do you think Japan is so frequently called out for doing this? Is historical revision a fact of every government? With the availability of books, media, and the Internet, it is easy to locate information that contradicts "official" versions of history. Why do you suppose the Japanese government—any government, really—engages in rewriting the past when such efforts are so readily debunked? Does it matter what the Japanese government declares to be history if everyone else knows otherwise and openly says so? Explain.

2. Many Japanese handicrafts and traditional manufacturing methods are dying out with their practitioners, although many of the objects are still in production (albeit with modern methods), and many of the rituals and traditions that use the objects are still being practiced. Does it matter if a kimono, for example, is made in China by a machine if Japanese people still own them and wear them to their cherished ceremonies? If a mechanized loom for weaving silk cloth could be sent back through time two hundred years, how do you think kimono manufacturers would have reacted? To what extent does modernization undermine or enhance traditional arts and crafts? Explain your answers.

Organizations to Contact

The editors have compiled the following list of organizations concerned with the issues debated in this book. The descriptions are derived from materials provided by the organizations. All have publications or information available for interested readers. The list was compiled on the date of publication of the present volume; the information provided here may change. Be aware that many organizations take several weeks or longer to respond to inquiries, so allow as much time as possible.

Japan Center for International Exchange (JCIE)
JCIE/USA, New York, NY 10016
(212) 679-4130 • fax: (212) 679-8410
e-mail: info@jcie.org
Web site: www.jcie.or.jp

With headquarters in Tokyo, the JCIE is one of the few independent nongovernmental organizations in the field of international affairs in Japan. The JCIE is dedicated to promoting Japan's engagement in the international community, encouraging thoughtful and collaborative analysis of critical issues in international affairs, strengthening civil society, and enhancing Japan's domestic and global contributions as well as establishing, strengthening, and expanding dialogue and cooperation. The JCIE does not take policy positions. It receives no government subsidies; rather, funding comes from private foundation grants, individual and corporate contributions, and contracts. It also publishes books on a wide variety of topics in international relations. The contact information given above is for its American affiliate, JCIE/USA.

Japan Civil Liberties Union (JCLU)

306 Atagoyama Bengoshi Bldg., 1-6-7 Atago, Minato-ku
Tokyo 105-0002
(81) 3-3437-6989 • fax: (81) 3-3578-6687
e-mail: jclu@jclu.org
Web site: www.jclu.org

The JCLU is an independent, nonprofit organization that aims to protect and promote human rights for all people regardless of beliefs, religion, or political opinion. JCLU's work is conducted in accordance with internationally recognized human rights principles, namely the United Nation's Universal Declaration of Human Rights. The JCLU frequently issues advice, memoranda, and opinions on specific human rights cases relating to activities of the national and local governments, the Diet, and the courts of Japan. In addition, it has led movements for new domestic legislation and ratification of the international human rights treaties by the Japanese government. The JCLU organizes seminars, meetings, and symposia; conducts research; and publishes reports, books, and newsletters, including an annual compilation of each year's articles, *Universal Principle*, which is presented in English.

Japan External Trade Organization (JETRO)

JETRO USA, 201 Third St., Ste. 1010
San Francisco, CA 94103
(415) 392-1333 • fax: (415) 788-6927
Web site: www.jetro.org

JETRO USA is the North American affiliate of the Japanese organization, which works to promote mutual trade and investment between Japan and the rest of the world. Established in 1958 to promote Japanese exports abroad, JETRO's focus for the twenty-first century has shifted toward promoting foreign direct investment into Japan and helping small to medium-sized Japanese firms maximize their global export potential. JETRO also publishes books and other resources for international company owners interested in doing business in Japan. JETRO USA has offices in Atlanta, Chicago, Houston, Los Angeles, New York City, and San Francisco.

Japan for Sustainability (JFS)

e-mail: info@japanfs.org
Web site: www.japanfs.org

The JFP is a nonprofit environmental communication service
that provides information about environmental sustainability
in Japan and the rest of the world, as well as information
about traditional wisdom and local activities of people working toward that goal. Via partnerships and open discourse, the
JFP hopes to bridge the gap between current and more sustainable behaviors, in developed and developing countries.
The group publishes a free monthly electronic newsletter and
runs the Daiwa-JFP Sustainability College (with its partner,
Daiwa Securities Group) to boost awareness of environmental
issues and facilitate action in the next generation of Japanese
leaders.

Japan Information and Cultural Center (JICC)

1155 21st St. NW, Washington, DC 20036-3308
(202) 238-6949 • fax: (202) 822-6524
e-mail: jicc@embjapan.org
Web site: www.us.emb-japan.go.jp/jicc

The JICC is the cultural and public affairs section of the Japanese embassy in Washington, D.C. Its primary role is to promote better understanding of Japan and Japanese culture by
providing a wide range of information, educational services,
and programs to the American public. The area it directly
serves includes Washington D.C., Maryland, and Virginia; fifteen other Japanese consulate offices provide services across
the United States and its territories. The JICC publishes a free
electronic newsletter, *Japan Now*, which discusses current topics in Japanese politics, economy, and society.

Japan International Cooperation Agency (JICA)

JICA USA, 1776 Eye St. NW, Ste. 895
Washington, DC 20006
(202) 293-2334 • fax: (202) 293-9200

e-mail: us_oso_rep@jica.go.jp
Web site: www.jica.go.jp

JICA is headquartered in Tokyo, with offices worldwide. Its mission is to promote economic growth and reduce poverty in a constantly changing environment of interconnected developing countries by addressing the global agenda, reducing poverty through equitable growth, improving the governance within developing countries, and achieving human security by establishing development partnerships and enhancing research and the better distribution of information. JICA publishes the quarterly magazine, *Network*, which discusses current JICA activities and reports on worldwide projects; it also publishes a variety of reports and statements in Japanese and English regarding the effectiveness and statistical impact of its programs. The JICA USA branch serves as a center for collaborating with other relief organizations in North America.

Japan Organization for Employment of the Elderly and Persons with Disabilities (JEED)
North Tower, New Pier Takeshiba, 11-1 Kaigan 1-chome
Minato-ku, Tokyo   105-0022
(81) 3-5400-1600 • fax: (81) 3-5400-1638
www.jeed.or.jp

JEED promotes vocational rehabilitation services and the employment of people with disabilities and the elderly. It provides counseling and assistance to prospective employers and jobseekers, and supports the vocational goals of middle-aged and older workers. The group operates the National Institute of Vocational Rehabilitation in Chiba, Japan, and sponsors the International Abilympics, an annual symposium and exhibition for manufacturers and providers of goods and materials that assist the disabled.

Japan Organization for International Cooperation in Family Planning (JOICFP)

Hoken-Kaikan Shinkan, 1-10 Ichigaya Tamachi, Shinjuku-ku
Tokyo   162-0843
(81) 3-3268-5875 • fax: (81) 3-3235-7090
e-mail: info@joicfp.or.jp
Web site: www.joicfp.or.jp

In April 1968, the JOICFP was established under the Japanese
Ministry of Foreign Affairs and the then-titled Ministry of
Health and Welfare to conduct research on family planning
and maternal and child health in developing countries. It also
provides subsidies and other necessary assistance for research
and other activities for developing countries in Asia, Africa,
and Latin America. Currently, the JOICFP is working on programs that integrate family planning with improvements in
nutrition, maternal and child health, and parasite control.
Within Japan, the organization disseminates information about
general population issues and advocates for reproductive
health and rights.

Japan Medical Association (JMA)

28-16, Honkomagome 2-chome, Bunkyo-ku, Tokyo   113-8621
(81) 3-3946-2121 • fax: (81) 3-3946-6295
Web site: www.med.or.jp

Founded in 1916, and then reestablished in its current form
in 1947, the JMA's mission is to provide leadership for physicians and to promote the highest standards of medical ethics
and education to protect the health of all Japanese citizens.
The JMA performs a wide variety of functions, such as advocating health promotion and patient safety policies and strategies, advocating access to quality health care in local communities, and providing leadership and guidance to physicians to
help them influence, manage and adapt to changes in health
care delivery. The JMA publishes a monthly journal, *Nihon
Ishikai Zasshi*; a semimonthly newsletter, *Nichii News*; and an
English-language journal, *Japan Medical Association Journal*.

Japan Small Business Research Institute (JSBRI)
Sanbancho KS Bldg., Sanbancho 2, Chiyoda-ku
Tokyo   102-0075
(81) 3-3222-3431 • fax: (81) 3-3222-0240
e-mail: kouryu@jsbri.or.jp
Web site: www.jsbri.or.jp

The JSBRI is a think tank that conducts research, gathers information, provides information, and promotes association with organizations worldwide that serve the interests of small and medium-sized businesses. The JSBRI directly supports small and medium-sized businesses by conducting meetings for owners of small businesses to exchange information, promoting local industries, and managing support centers. The organization publishes books and collects literature about small and medium-sized businesses to make the sharing of information and research results more efficient. The JSBRI believes that investing in small and medium-sized businesses will smooth the path to future economic success.

Japan Student Services Organization (JASSO)
10-7 Ichigayahonmura-cho, Shinjuku-ku, Tokyo   162-8412
(81) 3-6743-6011
e-mail: kouhou@jasso.go.jp
Web site: www.jasso.go.jp

The JASSO provides scholarship loans to highly motivated students who have difficulties pursuing their studies due to financial reasons. It also collects and analyzes useful information on student support activities and provides information on student support in order to improve the quality of its programs by analyzing the needs of students at educational institutions. JASSO supports international students, too, by providing scholarships to students who wish to study in Japan, implementing international exchange programs, and administering the entry exams for admission to Japanese schools.

Japan Whaling Association (JWA)
Toyomishinko Bldg. 7F, 4-5 Toyomi-cho, Chuoh-ku
Tokyo   104-0055
e-mail: kujira@whaling.jp
Web site: www.whaling.jp

The JWA was first established as a nonprofit group in 1959 but was restructured in 1988 as a private organization. Its current goals are to effect a revival and sound development of the whaling industry by collecting, studying, and clarifying information about whaling and lobbying for the reinstatement of commercial whaling. The restructuring occurred after the International Whaling Commission banned commercial whaling worldwide. The JWA jointly publishes a journal, *Isana*, with the Japanese Fishing Association.

National Women's Education Center, Japan (NWEC)
728 Sugaya, Ranzan-machi, Hiki-gun, Saitama
   355-0292 Japan
e-mail: webmaster@nwec.jp
Web site: www.nwec.jp/en

The principal objective of the NWEC is to promote women's education and contribute to the realization of a gender-equal society by conducting training programs for regional government officers, educational and group leaders, international trainees, and other personnel in women's education, as well as by conducting specialized research and surveys on women's education. The NWEC publishes a newsletter and various research reports and hosts on its Web site a database of literature and statistics regarding women's education. The center was founded in 1977 as an affiliate of the Japanese Ministry of Education.

Refugees International Japan (RIJ)
c/o Showa Shell Sekiyu K.K., Tokyo   135-8074
(81) 3-5500-3093 • fax: (81) 3-5500-3094
e-mail: enquiries@refugeesinternationaljapan.org
Web site: www.refugeesinternationaljapan.org

RIJ is an independent not-for-profit organization dedicated to raising funds to assist refugees who have lost everything as a result of war and conflict. Operating out of Tokyo, it is staffed entirely by volunteers from the Japanese and international communities. RIJ channels project funds through experienced organizations already working with refugees out in the field, ensuring that assistance goes quickly and directly to where it is most needed. It publishes an annual review and an annual newsletter. Its sister organization is Refugees International, which is headquartered in the United States. Both organizations were founded simultaneously in 1979 in response to the large numbers of displaced people in Southeast Asia after a decade of war.

Bibliography of Books

David Arase — *The Challenge of Change: East Asia in the New Millennium.* Berkeley, CA: Institute of East Asia Studies, 2003.

Daniel Barenblatt — *A Plague upon Humanity: The Hidden History of Japan's Biological Warfare Program.* New York: HarperPerennial, 2005.

Thomas Berger, Mike Mochizuki, and Jitsuo Tsuchiyama, eds. — *Japan in International Politics: The Foreign Policies of an Adaptive State.* Boulder, CO: Lynne Rienner, 2007.

Joseph Campbell — *Sake and Satori: Asian Journals, Japan.* Novato, CA: New World Library, 2002.

Jennifer Chan, ed. — *Another Japan Is Possible: New Social Movements and Global Citizenship Education.* Palo Alto, CA: Stanford University Press, 2008.

Ian Condry — *Hip-Hop Japan: Rap and the Paths of Cultural Globalization.* Durham, NC: Duke University Press, 2006.

Andrew Darby — *Harpoon: Into the Heart of Whaling.* New York: Da Capo, 2008.

Roger Davies — *The Japanese Mind: Understanding Contemporary Japanese Culture.* Rutland, VT: Tuttle, 2002.

Mike Douglass — *Japan and Global Migration: Foreign Workers and the Advent of a Multicultural Society.* Honolulu: University of Hawaii Press, 2003.

Patrick Drazen — *Anime Explosion! The What? Why? and Wow! of Japanese Animation.* Berkeley, CA: Stone Bridge, 2003.

Alexis Dudden — *Troubled Apologies Among Japan, Korea, and the United States.* Irvington, NY: Columbia University Press, 2008.

Bill Emmott — *Rivals: How the Power Struggle Between China, India and Japan Will Shape Our Next Decade.* Orlando, FL: Harcourt, 2008.

Bruce Feiler — *Learning to Bow: Inside the Heart of Japan.* New York: HarperPerennial, 2004.

Andrew Gordon — *A Modern History of Japan: From Tokugawa Times to the Present.* 2nd ed. New York: Oxford University Press, 2008.

Timothy Hornyak — *Loving the Machine: The Art and Science of Japanese Robots.* Tokyo: Kodansha International, 2006.

Eiko Ikegami — *Bonds of Civility: Aesthetic Networks and the Political Origins of Japanese Culture.* New York: Cambridge University Press, 2005.

Lea Jacobson — *Bar Flower: My Decadently Destructive Days as a Tokyo Nightclub Hostess.* New York: St. Martin's, 2008.

Pradyumna Karan — *Japan in the 21st Century: Environment, Economy, and Society.* Lexington, KY: University Press of Kentucky, 2005.

John Knight — *Waiting for Wolves in Japan: An Anthropological Study of People-Wildlife Relations.* Honolulu: University of Hawaii Press, 2006.

John Lie — *Multiethnic Japan.* Cambridge, MA: Harvard University Press, 2004.

Alan MacFarlane — *Japan Through the Looking Glass.* London: Profile Books, 2009.

Laura Miller and Jan Bardsley, eds. — *Bad Girls of Japan.* New York: Palgrave Macmillan, 2005.

Minoru Morita — *Curing Japan's America Addiction: How Bush and Koizumi Destroyed Japan's Middle Class and What We Need to Do to Fix It.* Seattle: Chin Music Press, 2008.

Karen Nakamura — *Deaf in Japan: Signing and the Politics of Identity.* Ithaca, NY: Cornell University Press, 2006.

John Nathan — *Japan Unbound: A Volatile Nation's Quest for Pride and Purpose.* Boston: Houghton-Mifflin, 2004.

Kenneth Pyle — *Japan Rising: The Resurgence of Japanese Power and Purpose.* New York: Public Affairs, 2007.

Frank Schwartz and Susan Pharr, eds. — *The State of Civil Society in Japan.* New York: Cambridge University Press, 2003.

Robert Whiting — *The Samurai Way of Baseball: The Impact of Ichiro and the New Wave from Japan.* New York: Grand Central, 2005.

Kate T. Williamson — *A Year in Japan.* New York: Princeton Architectural Press, 2006.

Tomiko Yoda and Harry Harootunian, eds. — *Japan After Japan: Social and Cultural Life from the Recessionary 1990s to the Present.* Durham, NC: Duke University Press, 2006.

Michael Zielenziger — *Shutting Out the Sun: How Japan Created Its Own Lost Generation.* New York: Vintage, 2007.

Index

A

Acquired Immune Deficiency Syndrome (AIDS), 38

Acutelogic (image processing company), 116

Age demographics, 31

Ainu Cultural Promotion Law, 170

Ainu ethnic group
Diet (parliament) resolution, 165–167, 169–170
discrimination against, 166–168
as indigenous people, 169–170
present circumstances, 166
U.N. declaration *vs.* Constitution, 168–169

Ando, Momofuku, 72

Andon reporting system, 75–76

Anime Consortium, 83–84

Anime industry
box office receipts from, 82
as business blind spot, 80–81
cultural differences in, 85–86
foreign market adaptations, 83–84
global popularity of, 78–79
as intellectual property, 78, 81–82
as legacy, 86–87
marketing potential of, 79–80
quality issues in, 84–85

Article 24. *See* Japanese Constitution

Arudou, Debito, 50, 52–53, 62

B

Basic Law for a Gender-Equal Society, 47

Basic Measures to Cope with a Declining Fertility Society, 23, 25

Basic Plan for Gender Equality (Second Plan), 37–38, 41

Bellona Foundation, 90–91

Bernstein, Andrew, 136–143

Body Mass Index (BMI), 126

Bringing Foreign Workers Ruins Japan (Ono), 54

Buddhist temples/funerals, 139–142, 147–148

Bunka (culture), 99–100

Burakumin class, 153–154

Buruma, Ian, 161–162

Business turnover concerns, 122

C

Caloric intakes, 126–127

Career training for women, 38

Cartels of the Mind: Japan's Intellectual Closed Shop (Hall), 62

Chambers, Veronica, 107–114

Chang, Iris, 161

Childcare and Family Care Leave Act, 25, 28

Children/child issues
cash incentives, 26
childcare leave, 23, 25, 28, 32
expense of raising, 32
father's role, 23, 26, 32
government benefit allowances, 33–34, 38

health, 32, 38
labor shortages, 50–51
mother's role, 32, 34
population decline, 31–32
resident registration law, 52
social duties, 149
China aid programs, 160
CIA World Factbook, 104
Citizenship rights, 51–52
Class/caste system, 153
Commercial ban on whaling, 89–90
Committee on Elimination of Discrimination against Women of the United Nations report, 48
Conference on the Human Environment (UNCHE), 97, 99
Continuous Improvement process, 70–71
Corporate culture restrictions, 20, 118–120
Cosplay (costume play), 104–105
Culture/cultural issues
child raising, 32
corporate, 73, 79, 85, 118
diet, 100–101
entrepreneurship, 117
exercise, 129–130
fashion, 105
geisha, 180
of indigenous Ainu, 168–169
intellectual development, 58
population change, 34–35
prosperity, 172
purity of, 34, 68
tochi seed eating, 175
on university campuses, 60
whaling, 93–94, 97–100
Cyber-geisha, 180–181

D

Dating services, 27
Death rites. *See* Funerals; Pre-funerals
Declaration on the Rights of Indigenous Peoples, 166
Diabetes rate, 132
Diet (parliament) Ainu resolution, 165–167, 169–170
Dietary concerns
longevity, 14
obesity, 131–135
tradition, 127–129, 175
whale meat, 97–100
Dillon, Read & Company, 159
Discrimination
of Ainu people, 166–167, 170
caste system, 153–154
against foreign renters, 60
laws against, 47–48, 51–52
in universities, 59, 62–63
Divorce rates, 19–20
Downer, Lesley, 180–181
Draper-Johnson mission, 158–160

E

The Economist (newspaper), 115–124
Edo period, 153
Education of women, 38
Elderly healthcare, 33
Employer issues
health initiatives, 133–135
population growth plan, 28–29
See also Workforce issues
Entrepreneurship issues
business turnover, 122
cafés, 111–114

conformity, 117–118
corporate culture restrictions, 118–120
economic environment, 123–124
global prevalence rates, 120
initial public offerings, 122–123
jewelry design, 111
pension loss fears, 118–119
trend recognition, 121–122
venture capital, 117
women workers, 107–110
working mothers, 113–114
See also Anime; Kimono industry
Equal Employment Opportunity Law, 47
Ethnic/racial demographics, 104
Exercise and culture, 129–130, 135

F

Faiola, Anthony, 33, 171–177
Family Registry Law, 166
Family social model, 45
Fashion trends, 104–105
Feminist movement, 48
Ferretti, Jane, 30–35
Fertility rates, 23
Fingleton, Eamonn, 155–163
Food issues, 127–128, 134
Foreigner issues
    renter discrimination, 60
    student increases, 51
    trainee programs, 53
Fukuda, Yasuo, 50–51
The Funeral (film), 138–139
Funerals
    government role in, 137–138

religious privatization, 141–142
social networking and, 142–143
undertaker power/practices, 138–141
See also Pre-funerals
Fusae, Ichikawa, 48
Fuyou Family Club, 27

G

Geisha: The Secret History of a Vanishing World (Downer), 180
Geisha industry, 179–182
Gemma, Masahiko, 125–130
Gender issues. *See* Japanese constitution; Women's issues
Global Gender Empowerment Measure (GEM), 46
Gordon, Beate Sirota, 45–46, 48
Government involvement
    child benefit allowances, 33–34, 38
    Chinese compensation, 159–160, 163–163
    in funerals, 137–138
    health care standards, 132–133
    opposition to Article 24, 45–47
    population goals, 24–26
    support for entrepreneurs, 121–122
Graves and funerals today: From ancestor worship to funereal freedom (Kenji), 140
Griffy-Brown, Charla, 110
Grove, Linda, 60

H

Hall, Ivan P., 62

Haruo, Inoue, 142

Hayashi, Fumiko, 40

Health issues

for children, 32, 38

diabetes rate, 132

for elderly, 33

employer involvement, 133–135

government standards, 132–133

HIV/AIDS, 38

insurance programs, 20, 32

medical costs, 20

metabolic syndrome, 133

for women, 38–39

See also Dietary concerns; Obesity

Hesterberg, Rick, 70, 73–75

Hideko, Kageyama, 48

Hogei Mondai Kondankai, 100

Hokkaido Former Aborigine Protection Law, 167

Hokkaido Utari Association, 165, 167

Hongo, Jun, 51

Hori, Yoshito, 118, 122–123

Horie, Takafumi, 117–118

Horvat, Andrew, 167

Human Immunodeficiency Virus (HIV), 38

Human rights for immigrants, 52

I

Iceland whaling, 91

Ikariyama, Toshimitsu, 174

Immigrants/immigration issues

foreign renter discrimination, 60

foreign student enrollment, 57–58

human rights guarantees, 52

language barrier, 60

legal protections, 52–53

Liberal Democratic Party plan, 49–54, 50

opposition to, 53–54

population growth, 20, 34

training/employment, 50–51

university faculty, 57–58

Initial public offerings (IPOs), 122–123

Initiative on Gender and Development, 39

Inoguchi, Kuniko, 37, 41

Insurance programs, 20, 32

Intellectual property rights, 78, 81–82

International Convention for the Regulation of Whaling (ICRW), 96–97

International Whaling Commission (IWC), 89–90, 94, 96–97

Internationalization, 58, 60–62

Internet issues

anime growth, 79–80

entrepreneurs, 117, 119, 123

innovation techniques, 121

teahouses, 180

Inwood, Glenn, 94

Ishii, Atsushi, 95–101

Ishikawa, Matsuhisa, 85

Ishikawa, Shinichiro, 78–81

Ito, Joichi, 119, 123

Ito, Satoshi, 85–86

J

Japan Association of Securities Dealers Automated Quotation (JASDAQ), 122
The Japan Times (newspaper), 160
Japanese Constitution, Article 24
  gender equality, 48
  gender roles, 44–45
  government opposition, 45–47
  legislative by-products of, 47
  values *vs.* freedoms, 43–44
Japanese Whaling Association (JWA), 99–100
Jewelry design business, 111
Jidoka (quality at the source), 72, 75
Johansen, Halvard, 91
Jones, Randall, 123
Just-In-Time (JIT) manufacturing, 72

K

Kaizen (continuous improvement), 70–71
Kato, Tadashi, 165
Kawano, Satsuki, 144–150
Kelts, Roland, 77–87
Kenji, Mori, 140–141
Kimono industry
  business decline, 172
  demographic changes, 173–174
  outsourcing, 175–177
  traditional values, 173
Kitchens, Susan, 40
Kogure, Satoko, 42–48
Koizumi, Junichiro, 37, 162
Koizumi, Takeo, 93

Kokusai PR (public relations firm), 99–100
Komiyama, Hiroshi, 58
Korea relations, 67
Kurokawa, Nabuo, 19
Kuwabara, Toshikazu, 63
Kyoko, Nishikawa, 44

L

Labour market issues, 118, 122
Language barrier issue, 60
Leadership roles for women, 39–41
Legal issues
  citizenship rights, 51–52
  Diet (parliament) Ainu resolution, 165–167, 169–170
  intellectual property rights, 78, 81–82
  labour market concerns, 118, 122
  marriage, 20–21, 27–28
  "next generation" law, 23–26
  patent awards, 119
  population growth legislation, 23–24
  protections for immigrants, 52–53
  resident registration, 52
  See also Japanese constitution
Liancourt Rocks, 67
Liberal Democratic Party (LDP), 43–46, 50
Life expectancy rates, 19
Lolitas (fashion subculture), 105
Lost in Translation (movie), 15

M

Machimura, Nobutaka, 165, 167–170

Maiko (geisha trainee), 179–182
Makihara, Susumu, 134
Makino, Catherine, 167
Manufacturing industry, 72
    See also Kimono industry;
      Toyota Motor Manufacturing
Marriage issues, 20–21, 27–28
Masuda, Takashi, 116, 122
Matsutani, Minoru, 49–54
McCurry, Justin, 178–182
McNeill, David, 55–64
"Measures to Cope with a Fewer
  Number of Children Plus One,"
  23
Measures to Support the Develop-
  ment of the Next Generation,
  law, 23–26
Medical costs, 20
Meguro, Yoriko, 36–41
Meiji era
    caste system end, 153
    Family Registry Law, 166–167
    feminists movement during,
      48
    funeral rituals and, 137, 141
Metabolic syndrome, 133
Ministry of Economy, Trade and
  Industry, 27–28
Ministry of Education, 57, 62, 159
Ministry of Health, Labor, and
  Welfare, 24, 132, 134
Minomi (parts storage system), 74
Miyazaki, Hayao, 78
Mizuho Financial Group, 27
Morita, Minoru, 53
Moronuki, Hideki, 93
Muda (waste), 71
Multicultural rhetoric *vs.* reality,
  63–64
Mulvey, Bern, 57, 59

Munesue, Toshiyuki, 169
MXC (TV show), 15

N

Nakagawa, Hidenao, 50, 53
Nakajima, Mineo, 64
Nakamura, Akemi, 60
Nakayama, Akio, 52
Nakayama, Shozo, 164–170
Nanking massacre lawsuits, 161
Nationality Law, 52
"Next generation" law, 23–26
Nishijin kimono district, 172–174,
  176
Noodle manufacturing, 72
Norway whaling, 90–91

O

Oakland, Noriko, 110
Obesity
    modern dietary changes and,
      131–135
    rates by country, 128
    traditional lifestyle/diet and,
      125–130
Ogawa, Naohiro, 22–29
Oishi, Buichi, 97
Okubo, Ayako, 95–101
Ono, Goro, 54
Organization for Economic Co-
  operation and Development
  (OECD), 117, 123
Otsuka, Kay, 108–109

P

Patent awards, 119
Pension loss fears, 118–119
Perry, Matthew, 15

"Plus one" plan, 23
Poff, John, 71, 73, 75
Political isolation, 68
Population growth issues
    cultural changes, 34–35
    employer burdens, 28–29
    government goals, 24–26
    legislation, 23–24
    marriage market, 27–28
    rate of decline, 31
    retirees, 32–33
    social changes, 34–35, 68
    women and, 31–32
    young workers and, 32–33
Pre-funerals
    contemporary developments, 145–146
    vs. funerals, 145–148
    ideology of, 149–150
    practical value of, 146–147
    See also Funerals
Pregnancy expense, 32
Prevention of Spousal Violence and the Protection of Victims, law, 47
Prideaux, Eric, 139

R

Raicho, Hiratsuka, 48
Rakuten (internet shopping firm), 122
Religion/religious issues
    Buddhist funeral practices, 137, 140
    privatization of, 141–142
    separation from state, 137
    See also Funerals; Pre-funerals
Research-and-development (R&D) expenditures, 119
Resident registration law, 52

Retherford, Robert D., 22–29
"Retired Husband Syndrome," 19
Retiree concerns, 32–33

S

Sakai, Mariko, 164–170
Sakanaka, Hidenori, 50–51, 54
Sasaki, Takaaki, 169
Seiji, Mitsunobu, 84
Semmoto, Sachio, 119
Senauer, Benjamin, 125–130
Shimamura, Natsu, 175
Shimizu, Yoko, 111
Shinto, 141, 153
Silk industry, 172–173, 175–176
Singer, Rena, 131–135
Slow Work, Slow Life (magazine), 108, 112
Smith, Jack, 69–76
Snowden, Paul, 56, 59, 63
Society for the Promotion of Funereal Freedom, 141
Solomon, Charles, 78
Sophia University, 60–61
"Soul parks," 138, 141
Stronach, Bruce, 57

T

Takase, Naoko, 135
Takeishi, Akira, 121
Takeshi's Castle (TV show), 15
Takeuchi, Hirotaka, 118
Tampakushitsu (protein), 99
Teahouse Internet, 180
Tetsuya, Takahashi, 44–45
Tezuka, Osamu, 78
Tezuka Productions, 84
Tochi seed custom, 175

Toshiko, Kishida, 48
Toyota Motor Manufacturing,
  Kentucky (TMMK)
  achievements, 70–71
  assembly lines, 75–76
  business principles, 71–72
  Continuous Improvement
    process, 70–71
  efficiency, 74–75
  manufacturing process, 73–74
  training priority, 72–73
Toyota Production System (TPS),
  71–73
Treaty of San Francisco, 159–160
Tsunemoto, Teruki, 168

U

Ungai, Hosono, 141
Unit 731 (biological warfare research institute), 156, 162
United Nations (U.N.)
  Conference on the Human
    Environment, 97, 99
  Declaration on the Rights of
    Indigenous Peoples, 166
  Global Gender Empowerment
    Measure, 46
University issues
  discrimination, 59, 62–63
  foreign faculty positions,
    57–58
  internationalization, 60–62
  multicultural rhetoric vs. real-
    ity, 63–64
  reform obstacles, 58–59

V

Values vs. freedoms, 43–44
Venture capital, 117, 119

W

Wage gap, men vs. women, 47
The Wages of Guilt (Buruma),
  161–162
Waseda University, 56
Waste elimination concerns, 71
Whaling industry issues
  commercial bans, 89–90
  cultural argument for, 98–100
  generation gap, 93–94
  in Iceland, 91
  nationalism, 100
  in Norway, 90–91
  nutrition data, 92
  retail products, 89
  support for, 90–93
  whale meat consumption, 98,
    100
Wiseman, Paul, 26
Women's issues
  birth rate, 19
  career training, 38
  divorce rates, 19–20
  entrepreneurship, 107–110
  expanding roles, 38–39
  female leadership roles, 39–41
  feminist movement, 48
  fertility rate, 23
  geisha industry, 179–182
  gender equality, 41
  health care, 38–39
  marriage, 20–21, 27–28
  population growth, 31–32
  pregnancy expense, 32
  "Retired Husband Syndrome,"
    19
  wage gap, 47
  working mothers, 113–114
  See also Children/child issues
Woodard, Colin, 88–94

Japan

Workforce issues
  childcare leave, 23, 25, 28, 32
  corporate innovation, 119, 121, 123
  couples with children, 23
  foreign trainees, 53
  labour market, 118, 122
  population growth, 32–33
  R&D expenditures, 119
  wage gaps, 47
  See also Employer issues; Entrepreneurship issues
World War II compensation
  Chinese government and, 159–160, 163–163
  claim rejection, 156
  financial ability and, 158–159
  from Germany, 156–157
  media spin on, 160–162
  for prisoners of war, 157
  U.S. aid for, 162

Y

Yachi, Tomoko, 112–114
Yamada, Katsuhiro, 83
Yamaguchi, Yasujiro, 173, 176–177

Z

Zawacki, Tom, 70–73, 76